Whole Marri
in a
Broken Worl

Discovery House Publishers

Books, music, and videos that feed the soul with the Word of God

Box 3566 Grand Rapids, MI 49501

WHOLE MARRIAGES
IN A
BROKEN WORLD

*God's Design
for a
Healthy Marriage*

Gary Inrig

Whole Marriages in a Broken World
Copyright © 1996 by Gary Inrig

Discovery House Publishers is affiliated with RBC Ministries, Grand
Rapids, Michigan 49512.

Discovery House books are distributed to the trade by Thomas Nelson
Publishers, Nashville, Tennessee 37214.

Unless otherwise indicated, all Scripture quotations are from the HOLY
BIBLE, NEW INTERNATIONAL VERSION. Copyright © 1973, 1978,
1984 International Bible Society. Used by permission of Zondervan Bible
Publishers.

Library of Congress Cataloging-in-Publication Data

Inrig, Gary.
    Whole marriages in a broken world : God's design for a healthy
marriage / Gary Inrig.
        p.   cm.
    ISBN 1-57293-015-2

    1. Married people—Religious life. 2. Marriage—Religious aspects—
Christianity. I. Title.
BV4596.M3I57   1996
248.8'44—dc20   96-18449
                                                                       CIP

Printed in the United States of America

97 98 99 00 01 / CHG / 10 9 8 7 6 5 4 3

Contents

To
Janice and Jeffrey
Heather and Catalin
with the prayer that your marriages
might thrive
to your good
and God's glory

Preface

I stood at the end of an aisle, a beautiful young woman dressed in a magnificent gown on my arm, preparing to take the few steps that would change my life and hers forever. Today it was my youngest daughter, Heather. Eight months earlier, it had been my firstborn, Janice. For this moment I was her father, taking her to the man who was to be her husband. In a few minutes, I would be her pastor, pronouncing them husband and wife. For this moment, I clasped her hand and remembered holding her tiny fingers as a baby. All too soon the man she loved would be putting his ring on one of them. And there, at the other end of the aisle stood not only my daughter's groom, but her mother, beaming with pride. It didn't seem possible that so many years had passed since she also stood at the end of an aisle, about to become my bride. I had thought then that I knew what love was all about, but the love we now share is so much richer and deeper.

I have officiated at hundreds of weddings and, through the years, shared with many couples preparing for marriage. I have spent countless hours with couples whose marriage is floundering in confusion or being battered by conflict. But it feels and looks entirely different when it is your own children who are entering marriage. When Elizabeth and I were married, no one considered it necessary to give us premarital counseling. It was assumed that because we came from good families, were surrounded by models of stable marriages, and were committed to follow Christ, that everything would work out. Those assumptions were dubious then; they would be nonsensical today. All around us marriages continue to disintegrate at an alarming rate. It takes far more than good intentions to build a good marriage.

Building a solid marriage today in our culture may be as difficult as at any time in history. But God hasn't left us on our own. He has given us in His Word, the Bible, solid, life-affirming wisdom about how to establish and nurture a thriving, satisfying marriage relationship. This book is written with the conviction that the God who gave marriage has also given us the basic information we need. That information can be supplemented by the best insights of counselors, therapists, and researchers, but it is God Himself who establishes the fundamental principles that produce healthy marriages. For that reason, we will focus our attention on understanding the biblical truths that undergird marriage God's way. And we will discover that His Word is practical, pertinent, and penetrating.

This book would be impossible without the loving presence in my life of my wife Elizabeth. She has taught me many of the most powerful truths I have learned, not by her words but by her life. I am profoundly grateful. I am thankful also to many friends who have been a source of wisdom and encouragement. Special thanks are due to Ginny Otis for her careful work in preparing the manuscript and to the loving congregation and pastoral team of Trinity Church who have ministered to us so well.

My prayer for you as you read these pages is that God's Spirit will open your eyes to see the truths of His Word that will have transforming impact on your marriage and that He will give you a heart faithfully to follow Christ into a deeper understanding of a marriage lived to the glory of God.

1

Love Story

THE MEDIA CALLED IT "the wedding of the century." According to the Archbishop of Canterbury it was "the stuff of which fairy tales are made." So on July 29, 1981, hundreds of dignitaries crowded St. Paul's Cathedral, hundreds of thousands filled the streets of London, and hundreds of millions of people around the world sat in front of their television sets, interrupting work or sleep to share the spectacle of a royal wedding. The marriage of the beautiful young school teacher and the heir to the British throne captured the fancy of the world.

But what began with such pomp, pageantry, and promise has unraveled publicly and painfully until all that remains is an empty shell—two people living separate lives in separate places bound only by their children and the power of the monarchy. An industry has grown up around the death of the marriage—assigning blame and circulating gossip. Whatever the future holds for Charles and Diana, their tragic story reminds us that fairy tales don't end the way they used to: "so they were married, and lived happily ever after."

Some cynics tell us that what happened to Charles and Diana was inevitable. Marriage, they tell us, is a doomed institution, a relic of an outmoded era. In the emerging twenty-first century, long-range, healthy, and stable marriages will be as viable as saber-toothed tigers. The only alternative is to develop more realistic options.

At first glance, such an opinion makes sense. We are daily made aware of how difficult marriage in the 1990s is. We encounter spiraling divorce rates, dysfunctional families, abusive relationships, "alternative" living arrangements, and homosexual partnerships. There are times when the media makes it appear that traditional marriage no longer works and something (or anything) must take its place. This may, in fact, be the most challenging time and culture in history in which to build a marriage that not only endures but becomes a source of love, fulfillment, and growth.

However, such marriages are not only possible but essential. The answer to the onslaught is not to be found in the reinvention of marriage but in the recovery of biblical marriage. Stable, thriving, satisfying marriages are possible if they are built upon the essential truths of God's Word by people willing to follow Christ consistently. There are no pat formulae or magic solutions. But there are hard answers for those who are willing to follow Christ in consistent obedience. Sometimes He will lead us counterculture. Other times He will lead us counter-tradition. But He is always leading us toward a relationship that reflects His eternal purpose for marriage.

One of the most striking biblical truths about marriage is that it is meant to be a portrayal of the greatest relationship in creation—the relationship between God and His people. Nothing could invest marriage with greater dignity or deeper significance than that comparison. Most often, when we think of that picture, we begin with what we have seen (human marriage) and try to understand the greater truth—the relation between Christ and His church. But our world doesn't present us with many healthy models of marriage. Therefore, in a world as confused as ours is about marriage, it is helpful to reverse the process: to look at the relationship between Christ and the church for what it can teach us about the relationship between husband and wife. That is clearly Paul's intention in his greatest statement about marriage—Ephesians 5:21–33, and as we begin, we want to look at his picture in the broadest sense, to gain a concept of what God sees as the essential ingredients of a thriving, healthy relationship.

> *Submit to one another out of reverence for Christ. Wives, submit to your husbands as to the Lord. For the husband is the head of the wife as Christ is the head of the church, his body, of which he is the Savior. Now as the church submits to Christ, so also wives should submit to their husbands in everything.*
>
> *Husbands, love your wives, just as Christ loved the church and gave himself up for her to make her holy, cleansing her by the washing with water through the word, and to present her to himself as a radiant church, without stain or wrinkle or any other blemish, but holy and blameless. In this same way, husbands ought to love their wives as their own bodies. He who loves his wife loves himself. After all, no one ever hated his own body, but he feeds and cares for it, just as Christ does the church—for we are members of his body. For this reason a man will leave his father and mother and be united to his wife, and the two will become one flesh. This is a profound mystery—but I am talking about Christ and the church. However, each one of you also must love his wife as he loves himself, and the wife must respect her husband.* (Ephesians 5:21–33)

Bookstore shelves are full of books on marriage, many of them describing the reasons marriages fail. Such books are usually written by therapists, who spend their time working with clients whose marriages are experiencing meltdown. A great deal can obviously be learned from marital pathology. We need to know why marriages fail. But the absence of death doesn't mean the presence of health. Many marriages are sick but never die in divorce or separation. So the most important question is why some marriages thrive and enjoy vigorous good health. Models of success are priceless in a world filled with failures. That is where Ephesians 5 helps us, by illuminating three essential qualities of a thriving marriage.

A THRIVING MARRIAGE EXPRESSES CHRISTLIKE LOVE

To say that a thriving marriage expresses love is a truism, even a platitude. But the essential question is, "What does love look like?" "What does love do?" That is the point at which Paul is so practical and yet so profound. The love that causes a marriage to thrive is modeled on Christ's love for His people, the church, and that love can be described in very specific ways. There are three distinct characteristics Paul discovers in the love of Christ.

First, Christ becomes for us the *pattern* of love, and that pattern is *sacrifice*. "Christ loved the church and gave himself up for her." Paul's focus is not on God's characteristic love for His people but on the specific love of Calvary: "Christ *loved* the church." This is important. It means that, in biblical terms, love is defined, not by the sweaty palms and beating heart of infatuated adolescents or the steamy passions of a Hollywood romance, but by the cross of Christ. Love produces sacrificial action. It is seen not just in what Christ felt but in what He did. "He loved the church and gave Himself up for her." The Lord Jesus was King of glory, Lord of heaven, eternal God. He could have given many things for the church, but He gave Himself, and that giving was based not on the church's merit or performance, but on her need.

The point is that *all that He has He gives for the church*. The love of Christ is the touchstone: true love means the sacrificial giving of self for the well-being of the loved one, whatever the cost to the lover and whatever the merit of the loved one.

I am overwhelmed by that. As a college student I met and fell deeply in love with Elizabeth. In many ways it was the easiest thing I ever did. I delight in her beauty, revel in her zest for life, and warm myself on her giving, caring persona. I find myself amazed at the privilege of sharing life with her.

But on a deeper level, loving her is the hardest thing I have ever done—not because of her, but because of me. Far too many times I want to love in a way that is comfortable and convenient to me. I want to love her for my good, not hers. I grew up in a family of boys and in a context of sports. It didn't take long to realize that the bantering humor and smart sarcastic rejoinders that worked well in the locker room didn't have the same effect on her. Over and over I found myself bruising her spirit with my insensitivity, and sadly I didn't even know it until I would find her hiding away in the university library, tears filling her eyes as she fearfully looked at the man she loved and wanted to trust, who all too often loved her in a way that met his needs, not hers.

I am still learning about the cross of love, thirty years later. Love gives itself up and gives itself away. It sacrifices—surrendering what it values for something it values even more. Sometimes the cost is trivial—the sacrifice of an evening watching a football game. Sometimes it is profound—the sacrifice of her availability and the financial cost of her going back to school so she can pursue a dream. But love means that I care for my partner more than anything else. A healthy marriage isn't about getting my fair share or giving my fair share. The cross wasn't about fairness. It was about need. And with the gift of sacrificial love I give the wonderful gift of *security*. "All that I have, I give for you, as Christ did for me."

Paul also wants us to reflect on the second characteristic of Christ's love, the *purpose* of love. Christ's love is not just powerful in its sacrifice, it is purposeful in its intention. "He gave himself up for her to make her holy . . . and to present her to himself as a radiant church." Christ's love is a transforming, empowering love. It comes to us where we are but it refuses to leave us there. It comes to us in our sin and unholiness and makes no requirement other than that we acknowledge those facts. But His love makes us holy. That means at least two things. To be holy is to be set apart, reserved for an owner and his purpose. I buy a pair of shoes and begin to wear them. At first they pinch and chafe and irritate my feet. The soles are too smooth and they slip easily on carpet or grass. But gradually those shoes are shaped to my feet and fit so comfortably that I hate to discard them and start over. In a special way, those shoes are holy. They belong to me and fit me and my purposes, and don't fit anyone else in quite the same way.

The Lord made us holy when He purchased us. At salvation, He sets us apart to be His people and, over the course of time, He is shaping us to fit His purposes. We were created to be this way, but sin has made us unholy. To become holy is to become what I was always intended to become—the realization of my God-given uniqueness.

The Lord also purposes to present the church to Himself as a radiant, splendid, glorious church. Paul is looking forward to the "wedding day," the culmination point of salvation history when the church, raptured and resurrected, is presented to Christ at His second coming. Imagine how we will look then—with all of the defilements and disfigurements and imperfections of this fallen world part of the past. We will be radiant in our new bodies with our renewed spirits, wearing the righteousness of Christ "without stain [of sin] or wrinkle [of mortality] or any other blemish [of fallenness], but holy and blameless [because of Christ]." That is the goal of it all—when you and I stand cleansed and qualified to be in God's holy presence. And it will be entirely due to Jesus Christ. By the sheer power of His love we will be transformed.

The Lord's love means that *all that He does, He does for the church*. His love is transforming, empowering, liberating. We are becoming what God intends.

There is a danger in pushing the illustration of Christ's love too far. After all, He is absolutely perfect and we certainly are not. Yet I am convinced there is an important lesson here. True love is empowering. We should not marry our partners to change them. Marriage isn't a reformatory. But the fact is that marriage will change us. No two people can live in marital proximity and be unchanged. The great question is, which way will they be changed? Will they be enlarged or diminished? Will they be enabled or disabled? Will they be empowered or exhausted?

I am convinced that if I truly love my wife, she will be empowered to become what God created her to be. Her God-intended design will become evident as she manifests her unique identity and the likeness of Jesus Christ. True love sanctifies and empowers—it enables the loved person to be what God intended.

It has done that for me. Elizabeth's encouragement has enabled me to do things I might have avoided, because I fear failure. Her insight has helped me evaluate myself and my circumstances; her godliness has deepened my trust in God. And at times I can glimpse things in her life that are there because I watered a seed of giftedness with encouragement and support. To live with an empowering love is to give the gift of *significance* to our partner.

There is a third way in which Christ models love. Paul sees in his relation to us the *provision* of love. "No one ever hated his own body, but he feeds and cares for it, just as Christ does the church." There is a double illustration here. We are sensitive to the needs of our physical bodies. We try to be wise enough not to cater to their desires but to respond to their needs. So when they are hungry, we feed them. When they are cold, we warm them (the words *care for* literally mean "to warm"). We value our bodies enough to treat them with respect. In fact, the care and feeding of the body in all its various forms is the main economic engine of every society.

In the same way, Christ feeds and cares for His church. He not only loved her enough to die for her, He loves her enough to provide her with all she needs. Two thousand years after Calvary, the church exists in every nation on earth, sustained, supported, and enriched even in the most difficult circumstances by the love, grace, and power of Jesus Christ. His provision is a daily experience for every child of God. *All that she needs, He provides for the church.*

The application to marriage is obvious. True love brings the gift of *support*, a sensitivity to my partner's personal, emotional, and physical needs. Unlike Christ I cannot provide all my wife's needs, but I can accept the responsibility to nurture and cherish. Marriages thrive when love is "fed." Marriages flourish when people are "cared for," warmed, and cherished.

What does love look life? It looks like Christ:

> *All that He has, He gives for the church,*
>   and in that gift of sacrifice, we find *security.*
> *All that He does, He does for the church,*
>   and in that gift of empowerment, we discover *significance.*
> *All that she needs, He provides for the church,*
>   and in that gift of provision, we experience *support.*

Christ loved the church enough to die for her, and that expression of love is indispensable to a thriving marriage. But there is another side to the illustration. The church responds to Christ's love. The church loves Christ enough to live for Him and in that response is the second essential.

A THRIVING MARRIAGE EXPERIENCES INTIMACY

Paul's description of Christ and the church employs another metaphor to emphasize the oneness that exists between His people and Himself: "we are members of his body." This is a favorite idea of the apostle. A relationship with Christ involves oneness—a unity not only like that of marriage but like that of the body. Our physical bodies operate on the principles of unity, diversity, and interdependence. In the same way spiritually, we are joined inseparably to Christ, made dependent for our love upon Him.

The union of Christ and the church is, in another way, like marriage. The body suggests we are dependent and interdependent. Marriage requires spiritual and emotional intimacy. Our unity with Christ does not diminish our identity. Christ will always be the Son of God—never less than that. And we will always be creatures— never more than that. We do not become "gods," neither do we lose our distinct personalities, as if the "bride of Christ" is one undifferentiated mass. Nevertheless we will share eternally in a dynamic, enduring intimacy with Christ.

Marriage has the same quality. A husband and wife are not simply companions and life partners, they are one flesh. In their union something new has come into being, bigger than either or both of them. There is "Gary" and there is "Elizabeth," but now there is also "Gary and Elizabeth," a new "being" which must be cared for, protected, and cherished. If this is forgotten, marriage descends into a living arrangement inhabited by two "married singles," who have aborted the "one flesh" God intends to create.

Peggy Noonan, who often writes with an insightful eye on modern culture, describes a conversation with a friend about life in the social circles of New York City:

> "Tell me about the marriages," I said. "Are those couples . . . in love? I mean, do they love each other?"

He said, "A lot of these marriages are deals. The marriage is a deal and you both do your part, whatever it is . . . . It's her first marriage, his second. They look good together, they love their children, and their marriage is about acquiring and appearing."

"Do they love each other?"

"No. The action for them isn't the love part, it's the having part. Having a pink-cheeked baby in the best stroller, in a hundred-dollar dress. Having an attractive wife or a handsome husband with graying hair. She's not interested in him anymore, and he doesn't really much like her. But they have a beautiful apartment on Park in the Eighties. They are a social and economic unit. It's a deal."

"Do they sleep together?"

"Yeah, it's part of the deal."[1]

Deals aren't just part of New York social life. Many Christian marriages are, in fact, deals. Couples have settled for a social arrangement that bears no resemblance to the model established by Christ and the church.

In a 1983 study two researchers wanted to learn how married couples and couples who are living together but not married handled decisions and resolved conflicts. Each couple was asked what they would do if they were given six hundred dollars to spend as they pleased. The researchers observed that married couples viewed the money as a joint possession and assumed they would decide together how to spend it. Cohabitors, on the other hand, viewed the money as something to be divided in two, with neither having the use of the partner's share. Most strikingly, the researchers observed that troubled marriages reacted like cohabitors. They viewed money, time, and possessions as personal property rather than as joint assets. That was "the deal."

In contrast, biblical marriage can't be reduced to a business arrangement. A one-flesh relationship isn't a deal, but a summons to oneness. Intimacy is not the creation of a moment, the product of a ceremony. It is the product of a lifetime, the process of sharing life. In the church's response to Christ we can see the basis of intimacy.

First, intimacy requires *unreserved trust*. The key to our relationship with Christ is confidence in His person. We are saved by faith, and we walk by faith. As we trust Him, we find that He is utterly trustworthy, and so we trust Him more.

Marital intimacy grows in the soil of trust and trustworthiness. Those two are inseparably linked. Marital intimacy requires and gives trust, and wise couples will do nothing that imperils the trust between them. When the writer of Proverbs celebrates the wife of noble character, he proclaims, "The heart of her husband trusts in her" (Proverbs 31:11 NASB). Remarkably, almost everywhere else in Scripture we are counseled to trust in God, not people. Marriage is a striking exception. Trust and trustworthiness build a safe place where intimacy thrives. A healthy marriage is a place of trust.

Second, the church responds to Christ with *unselfish loyalty*. She cooperates with His purposes. "As the church submits to Christ" becomes the model of marriage. The *s* word of submission is an unpopular one in the modern world, but it is the underlying principle of marriage: "submit to one another out of reverence for Christ." We will consider in a later chapter the particular way wives and husbands are to live out that submission, but the church's model is clear. We actively pursue Christ's goals and purposes. The only alternative is another, far more sinister *s* word, "selfishness."

Marriage forces us to choose the *s* word that will be our operating principle. Selfishness or submission—there are no third options. In the final analysis, we are called to the active pursuit of God's goals and purposes, an unselfish loyalty to this one-flesh commitment which means we put into practice Philippians 2:3–4: "Do nothing out of selfish ambition or vain conceit, but in humility consider others better than yourselves. Each of you should look not only to your own interests, but also to the interests of others."

The third ingredient of intimacy is *utter respect*. The church lives out a commitment to Christ's glory. In an ocean of indifference and antagonism to the Son of God, the church exists to praise His name and promote His glory. We refuse to treat Him lightly or casually.

Marriage is meant to be an island of respect as well. The world diminishes people, uses them, or is massively indifferent to them. Yesterday's heroes are tomorrow's nobodies. The people who applaud you when you perform ignore you when you fail. But a couple reaching for intimacy refuses to take each other for granted or to affirm the world's indifference or antagonism. "I like you, I want you, I value you, I love being with you, you matter to me more than anyone else"—that is the anthem of intimacy. Healthy couples focus on what they love about one another and build on the positive.

There is a third principle embodied in the words of Paul in Ephesians 5. This moves away from the specifics of the relationship between Christ and the church and asks us to evaluate and embrace the values on which that relationship is based.

A THRIVING MARRIAGE EMBRACES CORE VALUES

First and foremost, a thriving marriage recognizes that *the resource for marriage is Christ*. We come to marriage as sinful and needy people. Because we are fallen people, we have developed sinful habits. Because we live in a fallen world, we have been sinned against and we have become victims of our own sin. As hurt and needy people, we all too often expect people close to us to meet our needs. But our needs are too deep for marriage alone to satisfy. All too many marriages fail, not because people expect too little of marriage, but because they expect too much. "He's the one." "She's the one who'll make me feel better." *But no person can do for us what only God can do.* If I ignore that, I am headed for inevitable disillusionment. If I operate out of my neediness, I will overburden my spouse. If I operate in my sinfulness, I will exploit and manipulate her.

That is why the cross is not only the model of love, it is the source of love. Only Christ can give me the forgiveness, grace, and power that frees me from the guilt and habits of sin. Only Christ can give me the love, peace, and freedom that enables me to be a giver and not just a taker.

Being married for almost thirty years is a profoundly humbling experience. In the course of time I have accumulated a huge inventory of failures, sins, and blunders. Yet Elizabeth continues to love me with a tenacious love. Clearly it's not because I'm so lovable. It has far more to do with the fact that she is loving. But I would have drained her supply decades ago except for the fact that she has an endless fountain of love through her relationship to Christ. Because of Him, there is always more for me to drink.

A second indispensable truth is that *the principle of marriage is grace*. This clearly follows from the first, since Christ is the fountain of grace. Strikingly, Ephesians 5:21–33 never uses the word *grace* but every verse is full of it. Christ responds to our need, not our merit. He provides all we need, not just a portion. The whole passage is rich in the picture of His compassion, kindness, mercy, and goodness. Grace means that we are accepted and forgiven.

Thriving marriages are grace-full. *Grace* means to accept and to be accepted. God doesn't put us on trial, making us walk a tightrope of performance so that one day we can reach a platform of acceptance. Grace-full partners give each other the benefit of the doubt and choose to focus on what they like about the other, rather than on what they don't like. Grace means to forgive and to be forgiven, a concept we will return to later because it is so important in a thriving marriage. Failure is inevitable because sinners are the only people who get married. Grace is the process in which two people who own their sin and failure and enjoy God's grace and forgiveness will extend the same to those who sin against and fail them.

A third core value embedded in Ephesians 5 is that *the pattern of marriage is ministry*. Again we face a choice. One way is manipulation—we use others to meet our needs. Living as we do in a culture absorbed with protecting rights and achieving self-actualization, it is easy to turn marriage into competition. But the way of Christ is servanthood, submission, ministry—the choice to meet needs. The Lord models for us that lordship doesn't mean personal satisfaction but personal service.

David Mace has observed that strong families are serving families. "The members of these families liked each other, and kept on telling each other that they liked each other. They affirmed each other, gave each other a sense of personal worth, and took every reasonable opportunity to speak and act affectionately. The result, very naturally, was that they enjoyed being together and reinforced each other in ways that made their relationship very satisfying."[2]

The problem with fairy tale romances is that they don't last very well in a hard-reality world. Charles and Diana's wedding was a marvelous spectacle for those who like such things, but life in the palace proved far tougher than pageantry in the cathedral. That is why the Bible is, from one perspective, so utterly unsentimental about marriage. We have turned the cross into religious unreality, a pious symbol stripped of its bloody brutality. Imagine carting an electric chair down the aisle immediately before the bridal procession or decorating a Valentine's card with a hangman's noose! But what Scripture forces us to do is to stand at the foot of the cross and confront its hard-nail reality. There, more clearly than anywhere else, I can see what love looks like and begin to realize the call that marriage places upon me. More importantly, it is there that by faith I experience the Lord of the cross and His love, and I am set free to share that love in my family. The cross is a love story that is no fairy tale, and its message does make it possible to live "happily every after."

2

The Master's Plan

An Irate Customer sent an angry letter to the offices of a "do-it yourself" company:

Dear Sir,

I built a birdhouse according to your stupid plans. Not only is it too big but it keeps blowing out of the tree.

"Unhappy"

A few weeks later he received a reply from the president of the company:

Dear "Unhappy,"

Please accept our apologies. We accidentally sent you a sailboat blueprint.

It may not be much consolation but, if you think you're unhappy, you should read the letter from the man who finished last in the Yacht Club regatta in a leaky birdhouse!

Even silly stories can have significant points. Whether the project is a birdhouse, a sailboat, or a new house, there are essential ingredients. You need a plan, the right materials, and competent workmen. Even those are not enough. No one begins to build an office building by dumping construction materials on an empty lot and setting to work with good intentions and high energy. When our congregation was building its new facility, our leadership team spent countless hours planning, researching, and working with the architect to develop an excellent set of blueprints. They were indispensable. But they were also insufficient, in and of themselves. We needed to do more than merely possess them. We needed to follow them.

Common sense tells us that a house is built by following good plans, purchasing quality materials, hiring qualified workers, and doing careful work. Even then, we have constant inspections and make continual corrections, because even the best blueprint proves inadequate, at some point. Good houses don't just happen. Neither do good marriages. Good people with good intentions with a good beginning don't always succeed. But there is a divine blueprint, that is perfect in its design and details, and points the way to success.

Proverbs reminds us of a basic fact:

> *By wisdom a house is built,*
> *and through understanding it is established;*
> *through knowledge its rooms are filled*
> *with rare and beautiful treasures.* (24:3–4)

God has given us the understanding and knowledge we need to build a thriving marriage. Wisdom means that we follow His directions. One of the best ways I know to get a handle on God's design is to go back to His original plan—marriage as He created it to be, as described for us in Genesis 2:18–25:

> *The LORD God said, "It is not good for the man to be alone. I will make a helper suitable for him."*
> *Now the LORD God had formed out of the ground all the beasts of the field and all the birds of the air. He brought them to the man to see what he would name them; and whatever the man called each living creature, that was its name. So the man gave names to all the livestock, the birds of the air and all the beasts of the field.*

*But for Adam no suitable helper was found. So the
LORD God caused the man to fall into a deep sleep; and
while he was sleeping, he took one of the man's ribs and
closed up the place with flesh. Then the LORD God made a
woman from the rib he had taken out of the man, and he
brought her to the man.*

The man said,

*"This is now bone of my bones
    and flesh of my flesh;
she shall be called 'woman,'
    for she was taken out of man."*

*For this reason a man will leave his father and mother and
be united to his wife, and they will become one flesh.*

*The man and his wife were both naked, and they felt no
shame.*

Not long after she received the Nobel Prize, Mother Theresa
made a tour of the United States. It was not a publicity or public-
relations tour, but a ministry-investigation tour. Reporters wondered
what needs she could expect to see in affluent America that could
compare to the grinding poverty and overwhelming physical misery
of India. Her reply caught them off guard: "Loneliness—the hunger
for human love—is the world's worst ill. People all over the world
are suffering more from loneliness than from poverty."

It is fascinating to bring that insight to Genesis 2. The context
is entirely different. This is not a world broken by man's failure
and inhumanity. This is creation as it came fresh from the hand of
God. In the sweeping panorama of creation given in Genesis
1:1–2:3 we see God's glory. "God saw all that He had made, and it
was very good" (1:31), and at the pinnacle of creation, He placed
humanity—man and woman bearing the image of God. The
creation account of Genesis 1 is a stunning account of the great
God bringing into being a state of affairs which fills Him with
delight. At the very peak of this creation stand a man and woman,
bearing God's image, sharing God's mandate to rule and fill the
earth, and experiencing the gift of human love in marriage.

In Genesis 2:4–25 we have, not a second account, but a different perspective on creation. So that we will not miss the significance of what God did, the author lingers. We learn that God did not create man and woman simultaneously, as we might have suspected from Genesis 1:27; "so God created man in his own image . . . male and female he created them." Rather Genesis 2 reveals that a process, a time interval, was involved. This delay in the creation of Eve after Adam was not an accident. It was divinely intended to reveal that the relationship between a man and a woman is unlike anything else in creation and also to unfold the divine blueprint for marriage.

MARRIAGE IS A DIVINE PROVISION FOR OUR GOOD

The Creator's words in Genesis 2:18, "It is not good for the man to be alone," come as a striking contrast to the affirmations of Genesis 1. In that chapter we read seven times that "God saw that it was good." Suddenly, for the first time, He declares that something in His creation is "not good." The Hebrew expression is particularly strong—it suggests that man's aloneness is the very opposite of good—it is "bad." Adam could look upward and enjoy a perfect relationship with his God. He could look down on the creation God had placed under his control and experience perfect harmony with his environment. But when he looked around him, his world was empty. There was no one who corresponded to him. And such aloneness was never God's intention. In fact, isolation kills. Studies reveal that people who have a sense that there is no one with whom they can share their personal feelings or have meaningful contact are twice as likely to get sick or die.

"Aloneness" is contrary to the very nature of God. The Trinity may be a mystery to us, but it makes clear that God Himself exists in relationship. And the God of relationships created people in His image with a need for relationships. We were never created to be self-sufficient or even dependent on God alone. This would sound almost sacrilegious, if God Himself had not said it. One of the most significant ways that need is met is within marriage. It is not the only way however. We need to read this passage in the larger context of divine revelation. We have a God-given need of and capacity for intimate relationships and opposite-sex relationships. This need exists whether or not we are called to marriage. Singleness is a gift of God, and if God has called someone to singleness, He has called them to something good. The Lord Jesus Himself did not require marriage to be a whole person. But we have needs for intimate (nonsexual) relationships with the opposite sex if we are single, and a married couple is called to embrace their relationship as God's gift.

Marriage is clearly portrayed in Scripture as God's invention. It is not the product of evolutionary need or cultural convention. Marriage matches the nature of man, as a social creature made in the image of God, and it accomplishes the purposes of God. To man and woman God gives His mandate: "Be fruitful and increase in number; fill the earth and subdue it. Rule . . ." (1:28). It was a tremendously exciting insight for me when I realized that God had not just called Elizabeth and me to team up to live with one another and for one another, but to team up to live for Him, as His kingdom agents. Marriage needs a cause bigger than "me" or "us" to realize its God-given purpose.

I am convinced that this is a dimension of marriage that is too often forgotten. Strong marriages have at their core a shared purpose which unites a couple's hearts, and that shared purpose needs to be linked to God's kingdom, God's purposes, God's glory. If our marriage isn't linked to what God is doing in the world, it becomes overwhelmed by the routines and trivialities of daily life or subverted by our sinful tendencies to pursue our kingdom and our glory. One of the reasons modern marriages are in crisis is because husbands and wives have been taught to do their own thing or, at best, to find "our" thing. Our deepest need is to do God's thing, to discover the unique way we as a couple can serve as agents of His kingdom purposes—to fill our world with His presence. Even in the Garden, Adam and Eve were given meaningful work to carry out together for the glory of God.

"It is not good for the man to be alone. I will make a helper suitable for him." Adam, God's image bearer, needs three things—a companion, a helper, and a completer. *For his aloneness, he needs a companion.* We need to distinguish between aloneness and loneliness. I may not be "alone" in the middle of a crowded room but I can be incredibly lonely. I have seen some very lonely people come together in marriage, believing that if they could end their "aloneness" they would also solve their loneliness. It doesn't work that way. Some of the loneliest people in this world are married people who share a marriage bed but not marital companionship. A wedding does not end loneliness, but marriage, God's way, brings with it the marvelous gift of companionship.

Adam also needed a helper because of his inadequacy. We could make a serious mistake here. "Helper" for us conveys inferiority. A carpenter's helper, a nurse's aide, a teacher's assistant—these denote relatively unskilled workers who handle routine chores to empower truly skilled workers. Is that what the woman is—a man's caddy and "gofer" who waits on him hand and foot? More than one chauvinist has delighted in that idea and mistreated his wife accordingly. But the word *helper* in Hebrew has a very different connotation, since it is most often used of the military assistance of a strong army, which comes to the aid of an endangered ally. More particularly, it is used of God Himself as the helper of His people. Nothing could make it clearer that *helper* is not a synonym for *servant* than the psalmist's celebration of God the Helper:

> *I lift my eyes to the hills—*
> *where does my help come from?*
> *My help comes from the LORD,*
> *the Maker of heaven and earth.* (Psalm 121:1–2)

> *We wait in hope for the LORD;*
> *he is our help and our shield.* (Psalm 33:20)

Clearly there is no sense of God as an inferior or secondary helper. In such contexts, a helper is one whose strength compensates for the inadequacy of another. A helper provides, protects, intervenes, and delivers. So, too, God intends the woman to be a person of strength whose resources correspond to the inadequacies of her partner. The reverse is also true. Marriage is a place of mutual help, where two competent but incomplete people empower one another.

Adam therefore needed *a complement, a completer of his incompleteness*. The Hebrew term translated "suitable for him" is especially rich. In its most literal sense it means "opposite to," but in the specific sense "corresponding to," opposite in the sense of completing rather than competing. Our uniquely male and female sexual organs obviously correspond to each other. But the correspondence between men and woman goes deeper than the physical complement. There are divinely intended gender differences that enrich life and empower one another. Men and women may be interdependent; they are not interchangeable. We will consider this concept of designed differences in later chapters.

There is a profoundly important concept here. Marriage requires difference to work well, because difference is the basis of synergy. Synergy means that the whole is greater than the sum of its parts. This was graphically illustrated in a recent agricultural fair. In a pulling contest, the two champion oxen pulled three times as much when they were yoked together as the champion ox had been able to pull on its own. Geese in formation are able to fly 70 percent farther than a goose on its own. Synergy multiples, it doesn't just add. There is a remarkable arithmetic to marriage. On one level, one plus one equals one, as Genesis 2:24 indicates. But simultaneously one plus one equals three or four. A good marriage doesn't simply add, it synergizes, bringing more out of each than either could have imagined. The whole is greater than the sum of its parts.

MARRIAGE IS A DIVINE PARTNERSHIP FOR OUR GOOD

Having announced the need for a partner for Adam, God might be expected to get on with the job of providing one. Instead He proceeds by a highly circuitous route. But the indirect route He uses to create Eve is, in fact, the most direct route to teach an important perspective on the nature of marriage. What follows is the divine drama of marriage, carried out in three acts.

The first act seems rather bizarre—a parade of animals and birds past Adam, who named each one (2:19–20). I have no idea whether Adam had any awareness of God's words in 2:18. Did God speak those words to him? Did God tell him he needed a "helper"? Whether He did or not, Adam must have sensed his aloneness, a sensation that would only have deepened as the parade continued. The beauty of those creatures would have stirred delight in him. Perhaps he was discerning enough to recognize that the strength of some creatures could be harnessed to aid him. But the fact remained: "For Adam no suitable helper was found." No creature corresponded to him. He had been created for relationship. Even God and His creatures could not totally fill His heart. There was a human-sized hole.

The naming of the animals was more than a feat of intellect; it was an act of authority. The concept of "naming" and "the name" is a rich one in biblical thought. When Adam named the animals, he did more than attach a label to them. He showed insight into their nature. And Adam named the creatures because God had called him to rule over them (1:28). In Genesis 1, God shows His authority as He names "day" and "night" (1:5), "sky" (1:6), and "land" and "seas" (1:10). But man, His regent, names the creatures. He is exercising God-given authority. This prepares the way for what will follow.

The second act of the drama involves the preparation and presentation of the woman (2:21–22). Adam is entirely passive, reduced to sleep, as God exercises His craftsmanship. Adam contributes the raw materials, but just as God had formed the man from the dust of the earth (2:7), He now builds the woman from the rib and flesh of Adam. Then, as the creator of male and female, He becomes the officiant of the first wedding, presenting Eve to Adam.

The third act of the drama is the poetry of marriage (2:23). "This is now" hardly conveys the intensity of Adam's words: "Finally," "at last," or "wow" come closer. "At last—bone of my bone, flesh of my flesh!" The spontaneous joy and recognition of Adam is obvious. She alone shares his nature and in her he sees a mirror of himself. In other creatures he saw God's creativity. In the woman he sees God's image and sees himself in a new way. Marriage is like that. In the intimacy of my union I see myself for who I really am. For Adam in the garden that moment was a delight. For me in my fallenness that mirror has often been profoundly disturbing.

"She shall be called 'woman,' for she was taken out of man." As Adam had done with the animals, he names the woman. But this time there is a profound difference: he gives his name (man, *ish*) to her (woman, *ishshah*).

What is this all about? What is God seeking to communicate by this unusual procedure? Why not create the woman directly and immediately? First, He is protecting *the dignity of the woman*. She is totally unlike any other creature. She is not property or a plaything. Rather she is an image bearer, created in God's image, created by God's hand, created for God's purposes. She is not Adam's aid, but his helper. Second, the process portrays *the leadership of the man*. The order of creation (first man, then woman) is said by the Holy Spirit to indicate that the man is to give leadership (1 Corinthians 11:3, 8–9). But that must not be overstated. Adam names the woman (authority); he names her with his name (equality). And it is Adam whom God holds primarily responsible for the sin of the first couple (3:9–12). The creation account thus portrays a delicate balance of loving leadership in a context of true equality. Third, the creation pattern of marriage reveals *the centrality of God*. From first to last, marriage is His idea and it is carried out in a context of perfect fellowship with Him. But when His centrality is denied, marriage becomes a source of suffering, brokenness, and rebellion.

MARRIAGE HAS A DIVINE PATTERN FOR OUR GOOD

When we come to verse 24 we have moved beyond the account of creation to the editorial comment upon the story. Moses may have penned these words but the Lord Jesus, in Matthew 19:4–5 attributes them to God himself. "At the beginning the Creator 'made them male and female,' and said, 'For this reason a man will *leave* his father and his mother and *be united* to his wife, and the two *will become* one flesh.'" The three verbs in this verse provide powerful insight into the essentials of marriage.

Leaving: The Bond of Priority Relationship

Marriage first of all requires *leaving*. The word is a strong one: "to leave, forsake, abandon." What is remarkable is that Hebrew marriages were usually patrilocal. That is, the new couple did not usually relocate away from the groom's parents but lived near or with them. The primary sense of the word here therefore is not *geographical* but *relational*. The new entity establishes a new priority, one transcending even the most significant of relationships. God requires that my relationship to my husband or wife transcend every relationship under God. My parents, my friends, my career, my ministry, my employer, my play things—all of these give way to a new loyalty.

We may marry because of feelings. We never marry by feelings. Marriage is based on commitments and promises, publicly taken so others can recognize my new loyalty. Marriage is therefore never simply a private arrangement of two people who decide to live together. It is always more—a public establishing of a new priority that rests on commitments. Feelings inevitably come and go. Commitments need not, and that is why a marriage endures by vows.

This means that marriage requires a change of lifestyle. In a society like ours where family ties are weak, we have a hard time imagining what it means to "forsake father and mother." But marriage inevitably transforms our attitude toward every other relationship we have. Some expect to enter marriage without significant change. But not only is that not possible, it isn't desirable. God insists that marriage be the priority relationship in life under Him. This requires choices and sacrifices. Our society tempts us to believe "you can have it all." Maturity recognizes that you can't. Biblical marriage means that I have made a covenant to surrender other options and loyalties because God has called me to an alliance, intended for life, with my spouse. My parents, my vocation, my friendships, and my ministry all have to find their new place under that new loyalty. If that choice is not deeply made, a couple is inevitably headed for trouble in their marriage. And when children enter the marriage, the couple needs to remember that even those special gifts of God must not be allowed to compete with their loyalty to one another.

Cleaving: The Glue of Passionate Commitment

The modern translation "be united to his wife" removes one of the great Elizabethan words that time has made memorable. The older version said, "He shall cleave to his wife." Unfortunately, the word *cleave* doesn't communicate much. I'm reminded of Beaver Cleaver of TV fame or a meat cleaver which cuts things in pieces. What does it mean to "cleave to your wife"?

The Hebrew word again is an especially rich one. *Dabaq* means "to stick, to cling." It describes the way flesh sticks to bones (Job 19:20) or the way welded metal is joined together (Isaiah 41:7). More personally it describes the passionate commitment of one person to another, beautifully illustrated in Ruth's loyalty to her mother-in-law, Naomi.

> *Ruth clung [dzbag] to her . . . [and] replied: "Don't urge me to leave you or to turn back from you. Where you go I will go, and where you stay I will stay. Your people will be my people and your God my God. Where you die I will die . . . ."* (Ruth 1:14–17)

It also describes the passion of a man for a woman:

> *His [Shechem's] heart was drawn to [lit. "stuck to"] Dinah daughter of Jacob, and he loved the girl and spoke tenderly to her.* (Genesis 34:3)

God's people are to stick to Him in loyal obedience:

> *Now choose life, so that you and your children may live and that you may love the Lord your God, listen to his voice and hold fast [lit. "stick"] to him.* (Deuteronomy 30:19–20)

> *My soul clings to you;*
> *your right hand upholds me.* (Psalm 63:8)

The call is therefore to passionate permanence. "To be united to my wife" doesn't simply call me to share bed and home with her.

It is a call to a relationship of exclusivity and emotional commitment. Our lives are to be linked inseparably as we give ourselves in ever increasing ways to each other. It is a command, not an automatic result. It means that I reject any pressure that could threaten or weaken our bond, and it calls me to strengthen the ties that bind us in every possible way. "Cleaving" means investing in my marriage by spending time, attending conferences and seminars, getting counsel, or whatever else is needed to maintain the "Crazy Glue" of marriage.

Weaving: The Process of Personal Intimacy

The final part of the verse, "they will become one flesh," is, first of all, a statement of sexual intimacy. Sexual intercourse is the closest to "one flesh" possible for human beings. The Bible is utterly unembarrassed by this as the following verse makes clear: "The man and his wife were both naked, and they felt no shame." Sex is not a consequence of the fall but a gift of God to His unfallen creatures, so that they might express and experience oneness. It is not an accident that *becoming* follows *leaving* and *cleaving*. God's place for sexual expression is, and always has been, within a context of permanent public commitment and loving emotional attachment.

But physical intimacy is intended to portray and enhance personal intimacy on every level. Sexual intimacy expresses a hunger for emotional intimacy. *Becoming* is an apt word. Marital intimacy doesn't just happen, it "becomes!" Having been in the process for about thirty years, I am aware of how far we've "become" and how much more we need to "become." The picture of a beautiful tapestry woven of two colored threads has helped me visualize this process. The beauty only comes into being as each thread retains its uniqueness but is woven together with and around the other so that something new develops. Two duplicate threads cannot weave a tapestry. But together two distinct threads can become a beautiful design. However, the weaving analogy has a flaw. Tapestries can unravel, and the threads can simply be reused in another weaving. Marriages can unravel too. But the threads are forever changed. Marriage is intended by God to be a permanent weaving.

Intimacy is a marital blessing. It is also a primary human need. Stress is an inescapable fact of modern life and it can have a deadly impact. There is a direct link between health and intimacy. Daniel Goleman, in his fascinating book, *Emotional Intelligence*, describes a Swedish study which showed that men under intense emotional stress had a death rate three times greater than people who said their lives were calm and placid. "Yet among men who said they had a dependable web of intimacy—a wife, close friends, and the like—*there was no relationship whatever between high stress levels and death rates.*"[1] Having a partner to share life with makes all the difference in the world. On the other hand, negative marriages make people sick, physically, emotionally, and relationally.

Someone once asked Rembrandt, "When is a painting finished?" His reply was, "When it expresses the intent of the artist." Genesis 2 is a wonderful description of God's intent for marriage—two people, each gifted but incomplete, giving themselves to one another in a leaving, cleaving, weaving relationship, and finding in each other companionship, empowerment, and synergistic completion. Is your marriage "finished"? That is, to what extent does it realize the intent of the Artist?

3

Trouble in Paradise

MARRIAGE HAS INSPIRED some of the oldest (and corniest) jokes ever told on planet Earth. I suspect that some of these, in somewhat different form, were part of the conversation of those who watched Noah build the ark:

"Marriage is like a bath—not so hot after you've been in it for awhile"

"Marriage is like a violin—when the music stops, the strings are still attached"

"A man may be a fool and not know it—but not if he's married!"

"A husband is someone who stands by you in troubles you would never have had if you hadn't married him."

"Marriage isn't just a word, it's a sentence."

"Marriage is the most expensive way of discovering your faults."

"The best marriage is between a deaf husband and a blind wife."

Abraham Lincoln, who knew firsthand about a difficult marriage, spoke for millions when he observed, "Marriage is neither heaven nor hell. It's just purgatory."

It's easy to laugh about marriage. But even the most insensitive can discern, beneath the laughter, an ocean of pain. No relationship has so much capacity for joy and delight or so much ability to inflict deep pain and suffering. Almost every other relationship gives us breathing room, a space to hide. But marriage requires that we allow another into the most intimate and personal crevices of our selves. It forces us to acknowledge the fortresses that we have so carefully constructed to protect or hide ourselves and to choose whether we will demolish them or maintain them. Either way, the choice involves pain.

Marriage begins with a celebration, full of hope, laughter, and love. We wear special clothes and invite special friends, who travel many miles to share our special moment. But so often, it disintegrates into an ordeal of pain, hurt, and misunderstanding. An anonymous poet paints the sad but familiar picture in a poem entitled "Walls" :

> Their wedding picture mocked them from the table, these two whose minds no longer touched each other.
>
> They lived with such a heavy barricade between them that neither battering ram of words nor artilleries of touch could break it down.
>
> Somewhere, between the oldest child's first tooth and the youngest daughter's graduation, they lost each other.
>
> Throughout the years, each slowly unraveled that tangled ball of string called self, and as they tugged at stubborn knots each hid his searching from the other.
>
> Sometimes she cried at night and begged the whispering darkness to tell her who she was.
>
> He lay beside her, snoring like a hibernating bear, unaware of her winter.
>
> Once, after they had made love, he wanted to tell her how afraid he was of dying, but fearing to show his naked soul, he spoke instead about the beauty of her breasts.
>
> She took a course in modern art, trying to find herself in colors splashed upon a canvas, and complaining to other women about men who were insensitive.
>
> He climbed a tomb called "the office," wrapped his mind in a shroud of paper figures and buried himself in customers.

Slowly, the wall between them rose, cemented by the mortar of indifference. One day, reaching out to touch each other, they found a barrier they could not penetrate, and recoiling from the coldness of the stone, each retreated from the stranger on the other side.

For when love dies, it is not in a moment of angry battle, nor when fiery bodies lose their heat.

It lies panting, exhausted, expiring at the bottom of a wall it could not scale.[1]

That scenario has been played out millions of times and may even be all too familiar as you read it. Why? What is the cause and what is the solution?

The most enticing description of marriage at its best is found in Genesis 2. The most penetrating analysis of why marriage can be at its worst is found in Genesis 3.

THE WAY WE WERE: MARRIAGE MADE BY HEAVEN

It is worth reviewing the essential truths of marriage, as God intended it, stated and illustrated in Genesis 2:24–25:

For this reason a man will leave his father and mother and be united to his wife, and they will become one flesh. The man and his wife were both naked, and they felt no shame.

Verse 24 simply but eloquently describes *the divine pattern*. Marriage involves leaving, cleaving, and weaving ("becoming"). It establishes a new priority, requires a deep loyalty, and anticipates a growing intimacy.

Verse 25 provides *a divine portrait*, the original couple naked and unashamed, experiencing uninhibited enjoyment of one another in God's presence. This is marriage as God intended it to be—free, open, sensual, and satisfying. But there is more here than an evocative picture. There are the essentials of marriage.

First, biblical marriage promotes *personal dignity*. The man and woman alike share God's image, have received God's creation mandate, and reflect divine creativity. The basis of their relationship with one another in God's presence is their personal worth as God's creatures. They have not received a handbook of carefully scripted roles and rules to guide their behavior. Rather, their relationship is built on enjoyment of and respect for one another.

Second, biblical marriage requires *practical ministry*. Adam and Eve are interdependent but not interchangeable. As man, Adam provides what the woman lacks. As woman, Eve supplies what the man requires. They are each intentionally insufficient but interdependently complete as they minister to one another.

Third, biblical marriage is built upon *perfect trust*. The foundation of any successful relationship is trust, and trust is the product of trustworthiness. Their open, unashamed nakedness is witness not only to their sexual attraction to one another but to their complete trust in one another. They do not fear each other. This is a critical factor in marriage. When trust is present, each person enjoys freedom. But when trust is broken, a relationship will replace freedom with control. A parent who trusts her teenager sets her free and feels free herself. But when she distrusts, she will try to control behavior by rules, duties, or guilt. Marriage is intended to operate on the principle of trust because its participants are trustworthy.

But sadly, Genesis 2:24–25 belongs to another world. We live in a Genesis 3 not a Genesis 2 world. It is impossible to exaggerate the importance of the event theologians call "the Fall." On its most basic level, the fall of man into sin is a historical event. Mankind really did lose its innocence at a point in time. On another level, it is a paradigmatic event, a vivid portrayal of the dynamics of temptation. At its most enduring level, the story records an event that explains the way things are and why, in a world created by God, we see so much that is in conflict with His character and purpose. If we do not take Genesis 3 seriously, we will be unable to understand our world, ourselves, our partners, or our marriage problems.

THE WAY WE ARE: DAMAGED GOODS

In Genesis 2 we learn that God gave Adam and Eve a simple but significant test. It was simple, so that they could not claim confusion: "You are free to eat from any tree in the garden; but you must not eat from the tree of the knowledge of good and evil, for when you eat of it you will surely die" (2:16–17). At the same time the test was significant. It was a call to trust God, to believe that He would give them the knowledge they needed, because He was good and gracious. As we will see, the essence of sin is a refusal to trust and obey God. It is therefore around that simple but significant test that the narrative now turns:

> *Now the serpent was more crafty than any of the wild animals the L*ORD *God had made. He said to the woman, "Did God really say, 'You must not eat from any tree in the garden'?"*
>
> *The woman said to the serpent, "We may eat fruit from the trees in the garden, but God did say, 'You must not eat fruit from the tree that is in the middle of the garden, and you must not touch it, or you will die.' "*
>
> *"You will not surely die," the serpent said to the woman. "For God knows that when you eat of it your eyes will be opened, and you will be like God, knowing good and evil."*
>
> *When the woman saw that the fruit of the tree was good for food and pleasing to the eye, and also desirable for gaining wisdom, she took some and ate it. She also gave some to her husband, who was with her, and he ate it. Then the eyes of both of them were opened, and they realized they were naked; so they sewed fig leaves together and made coverings for themselves.*
>
> *Then the man and his wife heard the sound of the L*ORD *God as he was walking in the garden in the cool of the day, and they hid from the L*ORD *God among the trees of the garden. But the L*ORD *God called to the man, "Where are you?"*
>
> *He answered, "I heard you in the garden, and I was afraid because I was naked; so I hid."*
>
> *And he said, "Who told you that you were naked? Have you eaten from the tree that I commanded you not to eat from?"*

> *The man said, "The woman you put here with me—she gave me some fruit from the tree, and I ate it."*
> *Then the* LORD *God said to the woman, "What is this you have done?"*
> *The woman said, "The serpent deceived me, and I ate."*
> *So the Lord God said to the serpent, "Because you have done this,*
> *Cursed are you above all the livestock and all the wild animals!*
> *You will crawl on your belly and you will eat dust all the days of your life.*
> *And I will put enmity between you and the woman, and between your offspring and hers;*
> *he will crush your head and you will strike his heel."*
> *To the woman he said,*
> *"I will greatly increase your pains in childbearing; with pain you will give birth to children.*
> *Your desire will be for your husband, and he will rule over you."* (Genesis 3:1–16)

Sin's Seductive Appeal: "You will be like God . . ."

There is much in this story that is significant but secondary to our purpose. Many of our questions are unanswered. How does a serpent talk? How does Satan use the serpent as his tool? Was Adam a spectator to the process? We can be sure that Satan came, as he so often comes, in a way that disguised his nature and his intentions. His appearance is not ugly, repulsive, or grotesque to Eve. Rather he fascinated and entranced her. And his temptation is couched in plausible-sounding half-truths.

It is extremely important that we understand the essence of his enticement, because it is a promise as relevant as tomorrow: "You will be like God, knowing good and evil." The irony is that Eve is already like God. She was, after all, created in His image and likeness. And she already knows good and evil. Good is what God says it is. Good is to obey God and evil is to disobey Him. Satan's real promise is, "You will be *as* God, *defining* good and evil."

Satan calls Eve to make herself the center of her universe, taking the place of God for herself. Rather than obeying God, she will become like God and the good will be what feels or looks good to her, and so too with evil.

This is the essence of sin—the replacement of God with myself. The root of sin is self-centeredness, and the root of conflict in marriage is the same. It takes an infinite variety of forms—from the militant, "I'll do it my way," to the pathetic, "Look how I'm hurting." But the cause is the same. God has been unseated and replaced on His throne by "I." Larry Crabb captures the seriousness of this:

> Self-centeredness is the killer. In every bad relationship it is the deadliest culprit. Poor communication, temper problems, unhealthy responses to dysfunctional family backgrounds, co-dependent relationships, and personal incompatibility— everything (unless medically caused) flows out of the cesspool of self-centeredness.[2]

Sin's Immediate Effect: The Shattered Image

When a rock hits a windshield at a certain angle and velocity, the glass doesn't break, it shatters. Although it retains its original shape, the window is totally affected by the event. No part of it escapes. So it was when humanity fell into sin. Theologians speak of the result as "total depravity." The expression does not mean that we are absolutely depraved so that no good remains and we are as bad as possible. Rather it means that we are depraved in our totality, in every part of our being. There is no aspect of our humanity that escapes the shattering impact of sin. God's image remains, but it is a shattered image, as the events of Genesis 3 indicate.

First, sin affects us *personally*. Immediately, Adam and Eve experience *a loss of innocence*. "They realized they were naked; so they sewed fig leaves together and made coverings for themselves." Their nakedness isn't new. Moments before, they had innocently and unashamedly delighted in it. But now they *feel* naked. Guilt and shame have been born within them and those two emotions live nestled in all of us. The fruit of sin is a distorted sense of self and a damaged sexuality, and each of us lives daily with the consequences of this choice.

Second, sin affects us *relationally*. As they look at one another, Adam and Eve experience a *loss of trust*. Their first instinct is to hide from one another, to cover their nakedness with loincloths made of fig leaves. The beautiful picture of 2:25 is replaced with the all-too-familiar picture of a couple hiding, covering, even cowering before one another, afraid to risk or to be vulnerable. Former generations may have feared physical nakedness. Ours abounds in nudity but cowers from emotional vulnerability, and we invest our energy in keeping secrets from one another.

Adam and Eve's second relational instinct born of the fall is to hurt and blame one another. Adam, because of his God-given assignment, is held responsible for the sin. But when he is challenged by God, Adam responds, "The woman you put here with me—she gave me." In a few words, he blames God and attacks his wife. As one wit put it, "Adam took it like a man—he blamed it on his wife." Or to quote another sage: "Adam blamed Eve; Eve blamed the serpent; and the serpent didn't have a leg to stand on." The words born in the garden are with us today: "You don't . . . you never . . . you always . . . ." Instead of open, unashamed nakedness, marriage becomes a win-lose contest of hiding and hurting. The garden had turned ugly.

Third, sin affects us *spiritually*. There is a tragic *loss of intimacy* with God. When God's presence is manifested, sinful man's response is fear and flight: "I heard you in the garden, and I was afraid because I was naked; so I hid." The fascinating thing is that this is the only time Adam has not been naked before God! After all, he has on his fig leaves. But fig leaves, of whatever kind, can never cover our guilt and shame before a holy God. So Adam not only fears and flees God, he fights Him: "the woman *you* put here with me . . . ." Adam indirectly blames God for his sin.

In the Northridge earthquake in Los Angeles early in 1994, one event stood out above the others. The first floor of an apartment building collapsed, and the second and third floors collapsed on top of it, bringing death to many and destruction throughout the building. In the Genesis 3 earthquake, the bottom floor of man's relation to God caved in, and man's relation to himself and to others caved in as well. Man's broken image inevitably leads to broken relationships. This is an eloquent reminder that our problems lie far deeper than anything marriage or moral resolve can repair.

Sin's Lingering Effects: The Battle of the Sexes

In response to sin, the Lord pronounces judgment on the serpent and proclaims the results of human sin on humanity and creation. There is also the marvelous promise that, through the woman's offspring, God will bring deliverance to humanity. This promise ultimately was fulfilled in the person of our Lord Jesus Christ. But it is in verse sixteen that the Lord makes it clear that man's greatest blessing, the marriage relationship, will not escape the contamination of sin.

First, the consequences for the woman are described. She will experience *mother trials*: "I will greatly increase your pains in childbearing; with pain you will give birth to children." The latter phrase literally reads, "with pain you will bring forth children." I suspect that the "bringing forth" involves not only the moment of birth, among the most powerful pains humans can experience, but also the pains of child raising. Physical pains can be limited; relational pains cannot. Many women know all too well that the physical pains of childbirth, powerful as they are, are far easier to handle than the heart pains of raising children in a fallen world.

The Lord also describes the *wife trials* the woman will experience: "Your desire will be for your husband, and he will rule over you." What does it mean that the woman's desire will be for her husband? The Hebrew word translated *desire* is found only two other times in the Old Testament—in Genesis 4:7, and in Song of Solomon 7:10. In the last reference, written by another writer perhaps 500 years later, the term describes a husband's "love-desire" for his wife: "I belong to my lover, and his desire for me." Some find that idea here: her relational desire for her husband makes her vulnerable to his exploitation. But in the judgment context of Genesis 3:16, the word has a somewhat different tone.

Moses uses the same expression in a very illuminating way in Genesis 4:7. As God confronts Cain with his anger because his sacrifice has been unacceptable, He warns, "If you do not do what is right, sin is crouching at your door; it *desires* to have you, but you must master it." Sin is pictured as a beast of prey, about to pounce on an unwary victim and devour it. The parallelism between the verses is instructive (literal rending):

3:16   *unto your husband [shall be] your desire*
        but he will rule (mashal) you.

4:7   *unto you [is] its desire*
        but you must rule (mashal) it.

The desire in 4:7 is a desire for dominance and control. What is suggested in 3:16 is that a woman will yearn to be free from the dominance of her husband. She will desire to gain the upper hand in her marriage.

His response will be to rule over her. This is not the loving leadership and the appropriate caregiving that God intended Adam to exercise. This is chauvinistic dominance, repressive male power, sinful lordship. History is eloquent testimony to the subjugation of women by men and the multitudinous ways Adam has used her and reduced Eve to service his needs and desires. It must be said very clearly that this is not marriage as God intended it. But sin-destroyed trust, and when trust is broken, control and power struggle to take its place.

The man experiences the fall in a somewhat different arena. To him, sin leads to chauvinism and to frustration in the area of work and achievement. "The ground . . . will produce thorns and thistles for you . . . . By the sweat of your brow you will eat your food" (Genesis 3:17–18). Man is by God's design a provider and a protector. But sin means that his provision for his wife will require a battle against thorns and thistles. Work becomes a source both of blessing and battle. Because men find significance in achievement, they will battle frustration and incompetence because of sin. They need a helper suited for them. But sin means they will often turn protection into exploitation and "rule" their wives. As a result, they will drive a wedge between themselves and the companion God gave to meet their loneliness. This loneliness is far more acute than that of Genesis 2. Adam's innocent loneliness was the result of uncompleted creation. Our fallen loneliness is the product of guilty choices, accompanied by a reminder that this is not the way things were meant to be.

The truth of Genesis 3:16 is played out in every home apart from the grace of God. Our marriages are not an exemption from the fall. They are often where its effects are seen most clearly. A husband and wife, called to be one flesh, find themselves tearing their oneness and one another apart. Sin has given birth to a self-centered spirit that wants to compete rather than complete, to control rather than trust. It is a problem that goes far deeper than the way we were socialized by our parents. The beast crouches in our marriages, ready to pounce and tear our "one flesh" apart.

THE WAY WE CAN BE: BACK TO THE FUTURE

However, Genesis 3 is at the beginning not the end of the Bible. The curse is not God's final word to us. All of Scripture points forward to the time when "the old order of things has passed away. . . . No longer will there be any curse . . ." (Revelation 21:4; 22:3). That ultimately points us to the new heaven and the new earth, but the entire story of the gospel is that God has acted and continues to act in history to deal with the curse. The New Testament doesn't support the curse, it reverses it. And one place redemption must be lived out is in our marriages. Genesis 3:16 isn't the will of God for marriage, Ephesians 5:21–33 is. In Christ, we are not only taken back to Genesis 2 to get a picture of God's original intention but forward to Ephesians 5 to gain an understanding of His ultimate intention for marriage.

• There is a new provision—the death of Christ, which deals with guilt and shame at the deepest level. The days of fig leaves are over.

• There is a new pattern—the love of Christ, which goes far beyond anything Adam in Genesis 2 had experienced, and puts a dagger into the heart of the power struggle described in 3:16.

• There is a new power—the Spirit of Christ, who internally empowers a man and a woman to live out the fruit of His presence.

• There is a new principle—the submission of Christ. The "win-lose" game of Genesis 3 based on hiding and hurting gives way to a "win-win" lifestyle, "for even Christ did not please himself" (Romans 15:3).

• There is a new privilege—the glory of Christ. Even the finest Christian family is not an end in itself. Marriage, marvelous as it can be, does not have ultimate importance. Only God does. So the chief end of marriage is to glorify God.

Our purpose in wading through some deep theological waters in this chapter has been to recognize that good marriages, no matter how well-intentioned we are or how hard we try, will never just happen. The effect of sin's entrance into humanity has been catastrophic. *The greatest destroyer of marriage is justified self-centeredness.* "I will be as God defining good and evil, doing it my way" has become the anthem of humanity. Our only hope is to come to the place of repentance, acknowledge that He alone is Lord and God, and determine, by grace, to do it His way. *The greatest need in marriage is forgiven forgivers.* Our sinful tendency is to live with guilt and shame, hiding and hurting our partner. But when we turn in our fig leaves, acknowledge our need of forgiveness, and clothe ourselves in the righteousness of Christ, something wonderful happens. We become forgiven forgivers, increasingly able to become "naked and unashamed" with each other. All of this is to say that *the greatest hope for marriage is Christ.* Genesis 3 makes it clear that Humpty Dumpty had a great fall. History tells us and experience reminds us that all the king's horses and all the king's men can't put Humpty together again. But the King's Son can and does. And that's why there can be whole marriages in a broken world.

4

Shutting the Back Door

A FTER DAVID LIVINGSTONE, the great nineteenth-century missionary-explorer, had been in Africa for about twelve years, he developed an intense desire to explore the country from the interior to the west coast. It involved traversing over a thousand miles of territory, uncharted by Europeans, but he saw it as part of his mission to provide a trail others could follow with the gospel. He knew it was not a journey he could make on his own. So he approached a local chief and asked him to permit twenty-seven of his young men to accompany him. The old chief had enough bitter experiences with white men and slave traders to be extremely cautious. Livingstone sensed his reluctance, and so he made a pledge: "If you give me your sons, I promise to return with them and deliver them to their homes and parents. My life will be a pledge."

The chief finally agreed and Livingstone and his party set out on what proved to be an incredible journey. They experienced dangerous animals, hostile tribes, difficult terrain, tropical diseases, and life-threatening circumstances. But finally, after months of arduous travel, they reached the coastal port. To his amazement, Livingstone found anchored in the harbor a British warship, sent from England to return him to London. The captain approached with the message: "Queen Victoria has sent me to urge you to come. All England is waiting to honor you, sir."

The temptation must have been overpowering. The prospect of home, honor, fortune, and fame enticed Livingstone, and the invitation of the queen was no small matter to a colonial Briton. But he had made a promise! The English naval officers scoffed. No white man was bound by a promise to an African, and how could a promise to a black chief stand against the request of Queen Victoria? But Livingstone disagreed. He turned his back on England and set off through the jungle to keep his word, finally returning two and a half years after he had made his promise.

The Africans never forgot that and they loved Livingstone for it. When he finally died, they insisted on burying his heart in Africa, although they returned his body to be interred in Westminster Abbey. They would listen to a man who kept his word. For Livingstone, it was a simple matter. What mattered most to him was a promise: "Lo, I am with you always, even to the end of the age" (Matthew 28:20 NASB). Livingstone called that "the word of a Gentleman" and he had staked his life on it. If he believed in a promise-keeping Lord, he must be a promise-keeping follower.

A Christian is simply a person who has taken God at His word, who has believed God's promise: "I tell you the truth, whoever hears my word and believes him who sent me has eternal life and will not be condemned; he has crossed over from death to life" (John 5:24).

We live in a society that views commitments as negotiable. Commitments are tentative because other options may become available. But Christ followers know that *commitments matter*. It matters to make them and it matters to keep them. And no commitment is more important than the marriage commitment.

The events of Genesis 3 permanently distorted the conditions under which we experience marriage. What God said was very good became very hard, because of the presence of sin. But the essential nature of marriage was not changed. It remains a covenant between a man and a woman, witnessed by God. My purpose in this chapter is not to expound on Malachi 2:10–16 but to think about the nature of marriage as a covenant. Yet it will be useful to have the prophet's words in our minds as we proceed. Notice his continued emphasis on keeping faith and the parallel he sees between Judah's covenant with God and the covenant of marriage:

Have we not all one Father? Did not one God create us? Why do we profane the covenant of our fathers by breaking faith with one another?

Judah has broken faith. A detestable thing has been committed in Israel and in Jerusalem: Judah has desecrated the sanctuary the LORD loves, by marrying the daughter of a foreign god. As for the man who does this, whoever he may be, may the LORD cut him off from the tents of Jacob—even though he brings offerings to the LORD Almighty.

Another thing you do: You flood the LORD's altar with tears. You weep and wail because he no longer pays attention to your offerings or accepts them with pleasure from your hands. You ask, "Why?" It is because the LORD is acting as the witness between you and the wife of your youth, because you have broken faith with her, though she is your partner, the wife of your marriage covenant.

Has not the LORD made them one? In flesh and spirit they are his. And why one? Because he was seeking godly offspring. So guard yourself in your spirit, and do not break faith with the wife of your youth,

"I hate divorce," says the LORD God of Israel, "and I hate a man's covering himself with violence as well as with his garment," says the LORD Almighty.

Two decades ago, John Denver wrote a beautiful song which captures the marvelous feelings a man and woman can share. He wrote it for his wife, and "Annie's Song" soared to the top of the charts. "You fill up my senses, like a walk in the forest . . . ." It's a song that still captures a mood for me. But it wasn't too many years later that word came that the Denvers were parting company.

Feelings are wonderful, but they are far too fragile a foundation on which to build a marriage. I thrive on the romantic feelings my wife and I share after all these years together, but in the crucible of life, it is commitment, not passion, that keeps us together. Our marriage is a covenant, established before God, and we endure and thrive in the knowledge of what that means.

UNDERSTANDING THE MARRIAGE COVENANT

It has become rather uncommon in our culture to speak of *covenant*. Perhaps the best way to explain what it means is to compare two ideas—covenant relationships and contract relationships—to understand the fundamental differences between them.

Contract relationships involve the exchange of services. They are based on a mutual arrangement between two parties. I supply goods or services, and in response another party supplies financial remuneration or compensating goods and services. In a contract, I earn what I get. And the relationship continues as long as the exchange is in effect or the compensation is satisfactory.

Contracts are entirely appropriate in their right place. It's exactly the relationship I want with my mechanic or local store. "You do your part; I'll do mine." But there are at least two places where contract relationships are deadly: with God and within our families. The problem with a contract relationship with God is that I can never, and will never, keep my end of the bargain. If I get what I earn, I will always receive judgment. Yet most people think salvation is a contract relationship: "I do my part; God does His." The transforming truth of the gospel is that it is a covenant relationship, based on the grace and character of God.

Contract marriages have become more common in an era of prenuptial agreements. The entire process is designed to make dissolution (and disillusion?) easier. We are told that the prenuptial contract between Jacqueline Kennedy and Aristotle Onassis had 170 clauses! Who wants a team of lawyers trailing you through your marriage, carefully tallying contract violations? But even that intricate document didn't prevent that famous marriage from being a sad failure. Contracts offer no real security.

When I was in an African country several years ago, I had a conversation with a doctor about the prevalence of abortions and unwanted babies in that country. He explained that young girls were valued as wives for their fertility. To prove this, many thirteen- to fifteen-year-olds would have "practice babies." I thought of that when I read a *Los Angeles Times* article which observed, "Gen Xers seem to be using first marriages as practice runs." The reporter pictured a bride in a Las Vegas wedding chapel, giving her weeping mother a thumbs-up sign in front of her new husband and shouting, "Don't look so sad, Mom! If it doesn't work, we can always get a divorce." Psychologists have begun to talk about "beginner marriages," and estimate that many in their twenties view their first marriage as a dress rehearsal for the one that really counts. One sociologist even calls beginner marriages "normal."[1] Sadly, they developed such attitudes from parents who treated their marriages as disposable contracts.

All too often marriage is treated as an unwritten contract in which partners record their spouse's contract violations. Some marriages are, in fact, *performance contracts*: "I'll do my part; you do yours." We're in this "as long as we both shall love," as long as the payoffs are satisfactory. But the contract may be revoked for nonperformance. "You just don't excite me like you used to." "I don't feel fulfilled in this relationship any more." This is a mindset that permeates our culture, and it makes all its practitioners tentative and uncertain in relationships.

Other marriages resemble *service contracts*. "I'll make you happy and you make me happy." "I'll meet your needs and you meet mine." The fundamental assumption is that another person has the ability to meet my needs, to fill my emptiness. But no human can do for another what only God can do. Other marriages resemble *maintenance contracts*. "I'll make you look good, if you make me look good." Public appearance becomes all important. You are to be my image enhancer, or image protector, whatever the realities of our private relationship. The contract reads, "Keep up appearances—that's your job," and far too many marriages operate on this arrangement.

Some marriages represent *remodeling contracts*. "I'll fix you" is one form; "please fix me" is another; "I fix myself and that'll fix you" is a third. "It's not us—it's you. Just go get some counseling, remodel yourself, and we'll be fine. You change, I'll pay." I've heard variations of that contract scores of times.

Contract marriages all work on the principle of exchanging services. And contract marriages produce consumers who continually ask, "What's in this for me," on the premise that one of life's supreme concerns is that my needs be met and someone else can do that for me.

Covenant relationships, in contrast, involve the commitment of persons. When God enters into a covenant, He commits himself without reservation. "I will be your God and you will be my people." He does not offer a part of Himself, or a service. A covenant involves the total commitment of the total person for the total life. So the marriage vow does not read, "I, Gary, take you, Elizabeth, to be cook, companion, housekeeper, and sexual partner." I entrusted my *self* to her, and she entrusted her self to me. That is the essence of marriage as a covenant. "I, Gary, take you, Elizabeth."

Marriage involves a *pledge commitment.* It rests on a vow, not just a promise. A promise can be fulfilled, and finished: "I'll take you out to dinner on Friday." Once done, the promise is over. A promise can be broken or be completed: "I'm sorry, but I've got a business meeting. I've got to cancel." But a vow is something different. A vow has continuing force. It can be being kept, but never "kept." As Mike Mason puts it, "To keep a vow means not to keep from breaking it, but to devote the rest of one's life to discovering what the vow means and to be willing to change and to grow accordingly."[2] For more than thirty years I have been keeping my vows to Elizabeth, but they maintain all their original power and force. We are pledged, not merely promised, to one another.

Covenant also involves a *personal commitment.* A vow is made *by* a person and *to* a person. Only a person can make a vow. For instance, our beautiful little poodle Danielle loved us. Her happiness was unbounded every time we came home. No one could doubt her commitment to us. But her affection was rather promiscuous. She loved anyone who would show her kindness. One day she didn't come back. We're convinced she was stolen by someone who lavished her with attention. Years later we still miss her, but she was incapable of making a vow of loyalty to us. But Elizabeth and I have made a commitment to one another. I am not committed to the institution of marriage—who wants to be committed to an institution? I am committed to Elizabeth.

Covenant also involves *a public commitment*. Marriage is not merely a personal arrangement between two parties. When God entered into a covenant with Noah, he hung a rainbow in the heavens so that His promise was visible to all. It is the very nature of covenant that it declares its commitments for all to hear.

Covenant entails *a permanent commitment*. God's covenants are unconditional, grounded in who He is. Without binding commitments people live in a land of perpetual adolescence, endlessly keeping their options open. Maturity requires the ability to make lasting, self-limiting, binding commitments. The reality is that commitment means letting oneself go, rather than tying oneself down. Every novice skier faces that moment of panic when the instructor insists that he put his weight on one ski. Everything in him says no. The snowplow position isn't much fun, but it does feel safe. But until a skier lets go and learns to commit his weight to the downhill ski, he or she will never be free to really ski. And until I enter into the reality of a personal, permanent, public pledge of myself to my partner, and live out that commitment, I am not free to enter into marriage as God intended.

BUILDING UPON THE MARRIAGE COVENANT

The vows that establish a marriage covenant are foundational to a stable, thriving marriage, but a healthy marriage requires far more than this. How we think about marriage will determine a great deal about what we expect from and invest in it. The prevailing model of our culture is therapeutic—marriage as a means to realize our "selves," to "grow," to actualize our potential, to love and be loved. Robert Roberts pictures this vividly:

> On this view marriage is soil. Its purpose is to help you grow sleek and wonderful, and make you like yourself very much. If instead your marriage holds you back and makes you small and withered, pale and dull and grumpy, then it's time to shake the old, depleted soil off your roots and repot yourself. The repotting may shock your system a bit, but you can hope that in a little while you will flower more than ever, and your deep green leaves will glisten. Of course, when the new soil, in its turn, runs

out of nutrients, it will be time to start over yet again. In this perspective marriage becomes a gentle (and sometimes not-so-gentle) form of mutual exploitation. There is no room here for lifelong promises: if you enter into a marriage for "growth," it makes no sense to promise to love and cherish your partner in sickness or in health, forsaking all others, until death do you part. If he becomes an invalid, that can put a cramp in the pursuit of your human potential. Or she may just become a dull person, or lazy, and then maybe someone more exciting will come along.[3]

There are a multitude of problems with the therapeutic model of marriage. But at its heart it is self-defeating. The Lord taught and lived by another principle—that we find our "selves" only by losing our "selves" and giving our "selves" away. "It is not good for the man to be alone" (Genesis 2:18), but "unless a grain of wheat falls into the earth and dies, it remains by itself alone; but if it dies, it bears much fruit" (John 12:24 NASB). The contractual model also embraces a fallacy—that another person has the primary ability and responsibility to meet my needs, and that the continuance of the relationship is contingent upon the satisfactory delivery of the services promised. "I haven't been happy with the quality of the bread we've bought here; I'll take my business elsewhere." "My needs just aren't being met. She (or he) is there for me in a way you've never been."

The covenant model is based on vows of permanence, the commitment of my self, and the establishment of a one-flesh relationship. It is not willing to settle for establishing stable social units, bonded pairs who stay together to raise children. It is not a deal. It seeks much more, a oneness that presses through the effects of the fall in pursuit of God's original intention for marriage.

Bound up with the concept of covenant is the idea of *covenant faithfulness*. One of the great truths of Scripture is that God is faithful. He acts in perfect congruence to His promises. He is undeviatingly reliable. Covenant involves trust. In my marriage vows, I gave my partner a claim upon me. I made a promise and invited, encouraged, even demanded her to trust me. I was twenty-three years old. What did I know of life or the future? How could I predict the things that would happen to me—to us? I couldn't and didn't. All I could do was pledge myself and ask Elizabeth to trust me—that I would be undeviatingly loyal to her. Amazingly, she did trust me—and I her. And that trust has nurtured us through the twists and turns of life. Trust is paradoxical. It is at once tough and fragile. When protected and kept intact, it is resilient, strong, powerful. "I trust her—she will never intentionally hurt or harm me." But take it for granted, presume upon it and violate it, and it can snap suddenly and be almost unrepairable: "I'll never trust you again."

That is why trust requires faithfulness—not just sexual faithfulness but personal faithfulness. Trust grows when the other person is trustworthy. We cannot and should not trust another person simply because they ask us to. We trust on the basis of good and sufficient evidence. Faith in Christ is not a blind leap into the dark, but a reliance upon His proven character and promises. So too in a marriage. Commitment produces faithfulness, faithfulness breeds trust, and trust leads to intimacy. No step in that equation can be omitted.

Another indispensable part of the covenant model is *covenant grace*. God's covenants are grace covenants, not performance contracts. Thus, one of the great covenant words is the Hebrew term *hesed*. It describes God's loyalty to His covenant commitments which is freely given in love. God established His covenants because of love and He filled them with grace. He is "the LORD, the compassionate and gracious God, slow to anger, abounding in love [*hesed*] and faithfulness, maintaining love [*hesed*] to thousands, and forgiving wickedness, rebellion and sin" (Exodus 34:6–7). He is grace-full. "Know therefore that the LORD your God is God; he is the faithful God keeping his covenant of love [*hesed*] . . ." (Deuteronomy 7:9).

Healthy marriage is grace-full. It does not turn a blind eye to sin and covenant violation, but it practices loving acceptance of one another, rather than performance acceptance. I cannot expect my wife to tolerate blatant sin in my life. Grace is not permissive. It does not merely tolerate or turn a blind eye. Rather, it is forgiving, and one of my great blessings is that Elizabeth continues to love me despite the many shortcomings she sees. Grace works by inner transformation rather than external control. And only God can work that transformation. As Jeff Van Vonderen wisely writes, "Always remember this: Under the best circumstances, the most healthy, most sensitive, most educated person is still not capable of meeting the needs of another. That is God's responsibility."[4] A covenant marriage is a grace-full marriage. It expresses open forgiveness rather than blaming and shaming. It values affirmation and encouragement. And, lest all of this sound too heavy, a grace-full marriage is full of fun. Grace couples laugh with, play with, and have a good time with one another.

Covenant marriages are empowering rather than controlling. They invigorate one another rather than drain one another. In fact, that is one of the most revealing questions I can ask about the state of our union: "Do our times together drain me or enrich me? Do they empty or empower?" I have a relationship with the person who delivers my morning paper that has been entirely satisfactory. I pay my money and I get my paper. I have no idea whether the person is male or female, young or old. It is a consistent, no-care, contractual relationship. But my marriage is a *covenant partnership*. I need to be a care-giver, and neither a caretaker (parenting my wife) or a care-taker (taking advantage of her). We have a restlessness when something comes between us and a determination to put it right. Covenants are high-maintenance items. They require continual attention to sustain their vitality.

VIOLATING THE MARRIAGE COVENANT

Counterfeit Covenants: Caring without Commitment
A marriage that is merely an empty shell is an ugly thing. Many have looked at such marriages and determined that duty-bound marriages that were legal but loveless had no attraction. Love and marriage should be natural, spontaneous, free. An older generation sang "Love and marriage go together like a horse and carriage." Recent generations have claimed that marriage kills love, and the number of cohabiting unmarried couples has spiraled upwards since the 1970s. In fact, the prevailing wisdom has become that a couple *should* live together before marriage. "What difference can a piece of paper make?"

Depending on the context, the answer is, of course, a great deal of difference. Written statements clarify and confirm commitments. I would not be at peace with a bank teller who told me, "We don't do deposit slips. Just give me your money," or a salesman who said, "We're not into receipts or contracts. Let's just trust each other." The problem is not that people who cohabit don't care for one another. It is that casual or partial commitment radically changes the nature of a relationship. Recently, for the first time in many years, we found ourselves renting a home. We were good tenants and respected our landlord's property. But it was her property, not mine, and I treated it as such. Were it mine, I would have made certain repairs and changes. But my interest was short-range. And so I withheld my money and my energy. When we purchased our new home, however, my attitude was completely different. I give careful and quick attention to problems, because it is ours.

I remember a young man who boasted of the freedom and genuine love of his live-in arrangement: "We don't need marriage. We're together because of love, not a marriage license." "Suppose you had a car accident and were paralyzed for life, what then?" I asked. "Would you expect her to stay? And what if it happened to her? How long would you be there, when it wasn't fun anymore?" His silence was eloquent. Counterfeit covenants always delete the hard parts. They are designed for summer, not for winter.

And there is another problem. They don't work. The rate of dissolution for live-in relationships is far higher than the divorce rate, high as it is, and the rate of disillusion is no less when separation occurs. The emotional trauma of separation is virtually the same as for most divorces. Furthermore, cohabitation turns out to be a very poor predictor of marriage stability. Couples who live together and who, presumably, pass the test and go on to get married have a significantly higher divorce rate than non-cohabiting couples. As David Myers notes, "Yet another myth crumbles. Seven recent studies concur that, compared to couples who don't cohabit with their spouses-to-be, those who do have *higher* divorce rates."[5] He cites surveys that show a 33 percent higher rate in the US, 54 percent in Canada, and 80 percent in Sweden.

Empty Covenants: Commitment without Caring

Far too many marriages are legal but loveless or lifeless. A man and his wife can live apart together, having made their vows, begun their journey but lost each other in the process. There are a multitude of varieties. Some marriages are mutually destructive. Others are quietly but painfully dysfunctional. Still others are outwardly respectable. There may be sexual faithfulness, but no personal intimacy. There may be financial stability but no emotional vulnerability. There may be polite respect, but no passionate care.

Lewis Smedes powerfully portrays one such empty covenant:

> I know of a man who makes a major moral production of his commitment keeping. He expects his grateful family to praise him with a morning hymn, "Great Is Thy Faithfulness," at every breakfast time.
>
> Everybody in town knows him for his moral character. He gets a loan from the bank, anytime, without collateral, on his reputation as a commitment keeper. Good old dependable Joe.
>
> He reminds Janine, his wife, of his selfless devotion to their marriage, reminds her constantly; it always gives him an advantage. His voice slides into the nasal register, bordering on a sneer, as he reminds her of how he has never given her reason to doubt his fidelity, though, God knows, he has had chances enough.
>
> He lets her know that he sticks around, not because she is worth sticking to, but because he is such a loyal character. So when he struts his commitment-keeping stuff, he ends up leaving Janine feeling like an unwanted woman who is cleaved to only because her husband is too moral to leave her.[6]

In Malachi we are left no doubt as to God's attitude: "I hate divorce" (2:16). But sometimes I have heard that read as if it means that He likes bad marriages. "All that really matters is that we don't divorce. We're O.K. if we stay together." But Malachi makes it clear that God's anger is directed towards those whose spirit is hardened and who break faith with their marriage partners, and their marriage vows. My vows go much further than saying, "I will not divorce you."

My intention is not to diminish concern about divorce. Rather, it is to increase our concern about empty marriages. God hates those as well. I wonder whether He does not feel about some marriages the way He felt about the church in Laodicea: "I know your deeds, that you are neither cold nor hot. I wish you were one or the other! So, because you are lukewarm—neither hot nor cold—I am about to spit you out of my mouth" (Revelation 3:15–16). The solution however is not divorce, but repentance.

Broken Covenants: Shattered Commitments

There is another fact that must be faced. Sometimes the behavior of a partner is so devastating that even vows as binding as marriage vows are no longer binding. The covenant is shattered. The subject of divorce is a controversial one and Christians have taken differing positions.[7] There is also a tremendous danger of adapting our beliefs to the prevailing cultural norms. The statement of Scripture is emphatic: " 'I hate divorce,' says the LORD God of Israel." Divorce tears apart what God has joined together and no divorce can please Him, because it is always the product of sin. Divorce is a covenant violation.

The situation addressed in Malachi was apparently one in which people sought divorce for the most trivial or selfish of reasons. For some, it was a matter of convenience, for others an opportunity for indulgence. Often the reasons given for divorce are a window into a sinful heart. A woman in Colorado ended her marriage because her husband made her duck whenever their car passed his girlfriend; a woman in Oklahoma wanted out because her husband was so stingy he made her wear his old false teeth; the wife of a soldier in New Mexico was forced to salute and address her husband as "Major"; a man sued his wife for divorce because his wife left a note saying she'd gone to play cards with the comment, "There will be a recipe for your dinner at 7 p.m. on Channel 2."

The Lord hates divorce because He hates sin and the hardness of people's hearts. But He does not require people to stay in a context in which a covenant violator is victimizing his or her spouse. Therefore, I am convinced that the Lord permits divorce and remarriage when one's partner has been sexually unfaithful (Matthew 19:1–12), or when an unbelieving partner permanently abandons the marriage relationship (1 Corinthians 7:12–16). I am inclined to believe that there are other violations, such as severe physical abuse, that shatter the covenant, as well.

But these exceptions must not cheapen our appreciation of our marriage vows or weaken our attachment to them. Christians are people who follow a Promise-keeper, and who, in obedience to Him, commit themselves to make and keep promises. It is in the environment of covenant that marriage flourishes.

Robertson McQuilkin served as the president of a growing college and seminary, and he was a respected missionary statesman when his wife was diagnosed with Alzheimer's disease. As the disease progressed and her need for care increased, he was faced with a decision. Friends advised him to institutionalize his wife so that she could get the care she required and so that he could continue to use his many gifts in God's work. But, full of common sense and personal concern as that counsel was, McQuilkin did not feel free to follow it. He resigned his position to devote full time to the care of his wife. His words are the words of a man who knows and values a covenant marriage:

> When the time came, the decision was firm. It took no great calculation. It was a matter of integrity. Had I not promised 42 years before "in sickness and in health . . . till death do us part?" It was no grim reality to which I stoically resigned however. It was only fair. She had, after all, cared for me for almost four decades, with marvelous devotion. Now it was my turn. . . .
>
> But how could I walk away from the responsibility of a ministry God had blessed so signally? Not easily. . . . Resignation was painful; but the right path was not difficult to discern. . . . Muriel is the joy of my life. . . . She is such a delight to me. I don't have to care for her, I get to.[8]

5

Developing Your Serve

O VER THE YEARS I've asked friends and acquaintances in different parts of the world a question that nearly always produces a stimulating conversation: "Without naming names, who do you know who has a thriving marriage? And what makes you think so?" Recently, I asked a group of longtime friends as we enjoyed a kind of reunion. We have a lot of friends in common, so the discussion was lively, even though the rule of anonymity was followed. We were all a little saddened at how few examples quickly jumped into our minds, and impressed at how similar the reasons were for those special marriages.

So let me suggest you do the same. Spend a few moments thinking about marriages you admire. What traits stand out? What characteristics seem to be common? What makes a marriage not just survive but thrive?

It shouldn't really be surprising that excellent marriages are a somewhat endangered species. That is exactly what Genesis 3:16 would lead us to expect. But Genesis 3 also helps us predict the answer. Thriving marriages are strong precisely at the points most significantly affected by the fall. Sin brought into being an every-person-for-himself mindset. Healthy marriages build on respect, support, teamwork, caring, companionship, and fun. In fact, I am convinced that *every great marriage will have in it two people seeking to live out God's principle of greatness.*

That principle is stated by the Lord Jesus in a context that never mentions marriage, but has everything to do with it. Christ the Servant of God wants us to recognize that servanthood is the secret of true greatness in every human relationship.

> *Then James and John, the sons of Zebedee, came to him. "Teacher," they said, "we want you to do for us whatever we ask."*
>
> *"What do you want me to do for you?" he asked.*
>
> *They replied, "Let one of us sit at your right and the other at your left in your glory."*
>
> *"You don't know what you are asking," Jesus said. "Can you drink the cup I drink or be baptized with the baptism I am baptized with?"*
>
> *"We can," they answered.*
>
> *Jesus said to them, "You will drink the cup I drink and be baptized with the baptism I am baptized with, but to sit at my right or left is not for me to grant. These places belong to those for whom they have been prepared."*
>
> *When the ten heard about this, they became indignant with James and John. Jesus called them together and said, "You know that those who are regarded as rulers of the Gentiles lord it over them, and their high officials exercise authority over them. Not so with you. Instead, whoever wants to become great among you must be your servant, and whoever wants to be first must be slave of all. For even the Son of Man did not come to be served, but to serve, and to give his life as a ransom for many."* (Mark 10:35–45)

Back in the days when stagecoaches were a major means of transport across the country, there wasn't much to choose between one seat and another. Inside was obviously better than outside, but stagecoaches were uncomfortable, crowded, and teeth-jarring, and they had a bad habit of breaking down or getting stuck in the mud. Nevertheless stage companies had first-, second-, and third-class fares. First class meant that when (not if) the stage broke down, ticket holders remained in place while others solved the problem. Second-class passengers were required to disembark, often into mud, but they watched while others worked. Third-class passengers had to get out, get their hands dirty, and help get the stage underway again.

It has always been a mark of success in the world that the first-class people are those who are served. Sometimes they purchase service with money; other times they demand or command service. But they are the entitled who enjoy power, privilege, and position.

The Lord Jesus Christ lived and modeled an entirely different lifestyle, one that challenges our prejudices and presuppositions. It has a direct application to our families. If we desire a first-class marriage, our responsibility is to commit to a third-class lifestyle, one that values serving rather than being served. That is a truth far easier to affirm than to practice, as the Lord's disciples discovered.

THE WORLD LIVES BY THE LOVE OF POWER: SCRAMBLING FOR THE THRONE

Not long before the event recorded by Mark in 10:35–45, the Lord had made a great promise to his men: "When the Son of Man sits on his glorious throne, you who have followed me will also sit on twelve thrones, judging the twelve tribes of Israel" (Matthew 19:28). Visions of glory and power had entered the minds of James and John, and the ancient serpent's seduction rang in their ears: "Go for the throne! Get as much as you can for yourself. Be like God." Why be content with one of the twelve best seats in the kingdom when the positions of special power, influence and prestige might be available? After all, the Lord helps those who help themselves. "If it's going to be someone, why not me?"

This is Genesis 3 full-grown. Justified self-centeredness became the rule of life, even in those closest to Jesus. "How will my needs be met, my pleasures be satisfied, my ambitions be served, my desires be fulfilled?" James and John see no need to defer to anyone else in their unholy scramble for the throne, and although we later read that the other disciples were indignant with the two brothers, I suspect it had more to do with jealousy and a feeling of being outmaneuvered than with godly indignation. The result is inevitable. A scramble for the throne inevitably leads to loss of trust and the beginnings of power games, competitiveness, and jealousy.

In any relationship there are two key issues—power and intimacy. In his helpful book *How's Your Family?* psychiatrist Jerry Lewis points out that power is the ability to influence another, while intimacy is the capacity to empathize with another.[1] As Genesis 2:25 beautifully illustrates, God intended both partners in a couple to possess high influence and deep empathy. But the fall so destroyed original intimacy and trust that by Genesis 3 we see the first scramble to control. That works itself out in a thousand ways in a marriage—some trivial and some extreme. At one extreme is aggressive, raw power—ugly physical and emotional abuse. At another is emotional manipulation and psychological controlling, often by powerful passive techniques. The gender politics that are so characteristic of the 1990s are, in many ways, simply the most recent manifestation of the scramble for the throne.

And once on the throne, power rules. "You know that those who are regarded as rulers of the Gentiles lord it over them, and their high officials exercise authority over them." The original language unfolds an interesting nuance in this verse. Power operates *down* on people. It lords it over by pushing them or putting them down. Secular rulers use position, brute force, legal coercion, or money to keep people down. And things in the first century were remarkably similar to today. As Karl Hess observes, "Voluntary giving of oneself in service of our fellow man is alien to Greek thought. The highest goal before a man was the development of his own personality."[2]

Over the years I have seen the struggle for power in so many forms, and I have been guilty of it countless times. I have seen wealthy men withhold financial information from their wives on the guise of "protecting her from worry," but in fact seeking to keep her dependent and controlled. I have seen sharp-tongued wives emasculate their husbands and sarcastic men devastate their wives' esteem. I have witnessed both men and women withhold sexually to control their partner and watched self-righteous, falsely spiritual partners load guilt and shame on their less-religious spouse. Blaming, attacking, withholding, withdrawing, demanding, deceiving, denying, coercing—these and more are the games power plays. And, to my shame, I've played them all on Elizabeth. But, high power and high intimacy cannot coexist. The throne ultimately is a very lonely place.

THE KINGDOM OPERATES BY THE POWER OF LOVE: TAKING THE TOWEL

The Lord Jesus teaches and models an entirely different lifestyle. He could not be more emphatic. "Not so with you." Those words should be put in bold block letters: "NOT SO WITH YOU." He utterly repudiates a lifestyle based on the love of power. Christians must not exploit one another, inside or outside of marriage. Christ followers cannot manipulate and dominate one another. Our attitude to the Lord Jesus must produce a revolutionary attitude to ourselves and others.

We are called to serve others, not ourselves. That is not to deny that we have legitimate needs in our lives that we must attend to. But we live in a therapeutically oriented "needs" culture that asks us to focus almost obsessively on our own needs. The result has all too often been a mind-set so focused on ourselves that we are blind to the neediness of others. Some needs we have don't require being filled so much as being emptied in loving service to others. Therefore the Lord calls us to see our responsibility more than our rights. "Whoever *wants* to become great among you *must* be your servant, and whoever *wants* to be first *must* be servant of all." The Lord does not condemn our wants, but He calls us to focus on our "musts."

One of the hardest things to achieve in life is balance. In recent years, the concept of codependence has received a great deal of attention. Sometimes it is used as a buzzword with little specific meaning. The term arose out of work with alcoholics. Therapists found that the spouses of such compulsives were often people who felt better about themselves if they were needed, if they were helping someone. So, they would often become caretakers, enabling the alcoholic and ensuring that he remained dependent on him or her. Codependents help because they need to be needed.

The response of some therapists was to insist that such people needed to refocus, to become self-indulgent, to get in touch with their own needs. "We are not here to meet other people's needs," they claimed. So suspicion was placed on almost all "helping" and "caring" behaviors. "Why are you doing that for him? Care for yourself first!"

Codependency does describe an unhealthy pattern of behavior. Caretaking and enabling out of a need to be needed is not healthy Christian love. Clinging, controlling self-sacrifice is not the way of Christ. But neither is narcissistic self-care and an obsession with oneself. There is a Christlike servanthood, a proper self-sacrifice, that finds joy in giving and caring. Codependence controls, servanthood empowers.

I have never been a rock climber. But in the years we lived close to the Canadian Rockies, I came to respect the skills and the mind-set of rock climbers.

El Capitan, a 3600-foot outcropping in Yosemite Park, presents special challenges, even to elite climbers. On July 19, 1989, a park ranger named Mark Wellman and his friend Mike Corbett set out to meet the challenge. The weather was brutally hot, the nights were cold, the winds were often intense. But seven days later Mark and Mike stood in triumph on top.

Well, only one could stand triumphantly. You see, Mark Wellman is a paraplegic paralyzed by a fall in 1982. At the time of the accident it appeared that he would never again participate in the sport he loved. But Mike didn't see it that way. So during the summer of 1989, Wellman used an eight-inch pull-up bar and a climbing device to pull himself up El Capitan, a feat of incredible strength and endurance. But it was Corbett who made it possible, driving in the pitons and securing the safety ropes. And when the rock near the top was too fragile to secure the pitons, it was Mike who put Mark on his back and carried him to the top.

Servants make it possible for others to do what they could never do on their own. "Two are better than one," Solomon writes, "because they have a good return for their work" (Ecclesiastes 4:9). But that presupposes that they are servants of one another. Consumer marriages ask the question, "What's in it for me?" Kingdom marriages ask, "What contribution can I make to you?" Power marriages use people; servant marriages build people.

Philippians 2:3–4 provides the operating principle of a servant marriage: "Do nothing out of selfish ambition or vain conceit, but in humility consider others better than yourselves. Each of you should look not only to your own interests, but also to the interests of others." These are verses worthy of careful study, but two things stand out. First, a servant promotes the dignity of the other. With a humility born out of a walk with God, he or she is able to respect and value the other. Second, a servant protects the interests of the other. This does not mean that we must ignore our own legitimate interests, nor does it require that we do whatever our partner desires. The Lord refused to yield to James's and John's request for a special seat, and He was not controlled by their expectations. But He was nonetheless sensitive to and concerned about the legitimate interests of His disciples.

It is significant that in Philippians, Paul immediately goes on to give the supreme example of a servant: "Your attitude should be the same as that of Christ Jesus . . . ." There follows one of the most moving and powerful descriptions of the Lord's life and ministry found in the Scriptures (Philippians 2:6–11). In Mark, the Lord puts himself before us as the model Servant: "For even the Son of Man did not come to be served, but to serve, and to give his life as a ransom for many" (Mark 10:45).

The Lord Jesus lived His entire life as a servant. He knew who He was—the Son of Man, the rightful heir of God's eternal Kingdom (Daniel 7:13–14). His servanthood was not born out of a sense of inferiority, but from a recognition of *infinite dignity*. He freely chose to do His Father's will, and that will involved not only becoming a man but living as a servant of people. He was not a servant of people's expectations. He did not cater to people's whims and demands. He did the will of God and did so with *infinite humility*. Most of all, He met His people's needs by giving His life as a divine ransom to set His people free from the power of sin and death. His death was a sacrifice. But a sacrifice isn't something discarded for no reason. When I put out my garbage, I don't speak of it as a sacrifice. We sacrifice when we give something of value for something we value even more. He gave His life for the joy of giving those He loved life and forgiveness. This is *infinite ministry.*

Sacrifice and servanthood have become bad words in the times in which we live. Outspoken advocates of self-realization, whose anthem is "I did it my way," have derided those who defer to their partners. The swaggering male has long mocked the man who chooses to pour himself out for the well-being of his wife. The militant feminist has heaped scorn on a woman who chooses to subordinate her talents and gifts to nurture her husband and children. And the result is all around us—an endless trail of broken hearts, broken homes, and broken children. But the love of power is a powerful call and many Christians have been seduced by it. Even many who claim allegiance to "traditional family values" seem more committed to "power marriages" than "servant marriages." Christ's call is to the way of the cross—the power of love, grace, and servanthood.

But what does servanthood look like in action? Obviously we cannot see a servanthood marriage modeled by the Lord Jesus, since He never married. But he does model a servant relationship, which can be seen in His relationship to Peter, and which has principles readily transferable to marriage.

THE LORD MODELS THE PATH OF SERVANTHOOD

1. *The Lord affirmed Peter's potential.*

"You are Simon son of John. You will be called Cephas [which, when translated, is Peter]" (John 1:42). Those were the very first words Jesus addressed to Peter. They were a statement about an unshaped, undeveloped peasant who was going to become one of the greatest figures in history. The Lord saw Peter in light of his gifts and possibilities.

Marriage partners have a choice about what they see in their partners. It isn't hard to find faults. But servant spouses choose to focus on what they like and value, to feed their partner's potential and to enjoy their partner's strengths, rather than exposing their weaknesses. They are cheerleaders for each other.

2. *The Lord was sensitive to Peter's needs.*

Jesus was a student of Peter, and He deals with him individually. He knows Peter is a man who needs a challenge, so He calls him in a unique way (Luke 5:1–11). He summons Peter to walk on water (Matthew 14:22–33), confronts his spiritual obtuseness (Matthew 16:23), gives him special insider experiences (the transfiguration and Gethsemane), warns him about his proud boasting (John 13:36–38), appears to him after his resurrection and Peter's denial (Luke 24:34), and gives him a personal reinstatement experience (John 21:15–23). The Lord was aware of what made Peter unique and treated him accordingly.

Servant spouses are students of their partners. They are acutely aware of their partner's unique temperament and personal history. They know what hurts and what helps. They recognize the unique way their partner feels affirmed and encouraged. Most important, they are not only students but servants. They act on the basis of what they know.

Gary Chapman makes the helpful observation that we express and feel love in a variety of ways he calls "love languages."[3] We express love in words, by deeds, by gifts, by time, or by touching. But our love languages aren't always the same. Suppose my love language is gifts but my wife uses words. A servant spouse realizes, "I can't just express love in the way I like. My goal is to make her feel love. Therefore, I need to express love on her terms, not just mine."

3. *The Lord was patient with Peter's weaknesses.*

Peter was impetuous, impulsive, and emotional. He had a knack for saying the wrong thing at the wrong time. He was brash, unpolished, unruly. But the Lord, disappointed as He might often have been, was incredibly patient with him. He almost never comes down hard on Peter, making ultimatums and demands that he "shape up or ship out." He chooses not to dwell on Peter's failures and shortcomings. Instead the Lord gives Peter room to grow and time to change.

A servant wife views her partner's weaknesses as one of the significant ways God has called her to be a helper to him. A servant husband is deeply and repentantly aware of his own weaknesses so that he is able to see his wife through eyes of grace, not judgment. The truth is that the very places I try to force change in my partner are the places she will prove to be most resistant.

4. *The Lord was gracious, despite Peter's failures.*

Mayor La Guardia of New York was once heard to say, "I don't fail often. But when I do, it's a beaut." Peter could relate. His failures were not the trivial shortcomings of the halfhearted. The Lord knew Peter would fail, and He clearly told him so. But when He was proven right, He did not abandon or attack Peter. Rather, He sought him in his failure and trusted him after his failure.

Our marriages are either grace-full or curse-full. As Jeff Van Vonderen points out in his excellent book, *Families Where Grace Is in Place*[4], grace lives when I realize that no human, however wonderful, can meet the needs of another person. Only God can do that. I am then freed not to be my partner's Source, but a resource who can help them come to the Source. Grace means I don't need to control or change or coerce my partner.

5. *The Lord was open despite Peter's dullness*

Even though he was with the greatest Communicator ever to walk on earth, Peter just didn't get it. When he was with the Lord at His time of greatest glory, the Mount of Transfiguration, Peter fell asleep. When the Lord was at His time of deepest need, in the Garden of Gethsemane, Peter fell asleep. In between he often seemed to be sleepwalking through Palestine, as time and again he misunderstood or misrepresented the Lord. But Jesus kept opening His life to him, sharing His inner self.

A servant spouse keeps opening her life to her partner, even when that vulnerability is costly or feels risky. I serve my partner when I share my self with her. The greatest gift I have to give is my self. Most men find this very hard. I often frustrate Elizabeth because I can be more disclosing from the pulpit than privately, alone with her. I haven't figured out all the reasons why that is so, but I do know that she needs me to open my inner life to her, and I serve her when I do so.

First-class marriages require a third-class lifestyle, the lifestyle of a servant. The scramble for the throne epitomized by James and John must give way to the stoop to the towel, modeled by the Lord of glory as He washed the feet of His disciples in the upper room.

Leonard Sweet, dean of the theological school at Drew University, tells of hearing a student complaining that he had been assigned to a rural parish. He was a city person who yearned for the stimulation of a city ministry. Why should he do rural ministry? As Sweet overheard his lament, he also heard his fellow student respond, "You know, the world's a better place because Michelangelo didn't say, 'I don't do ceilings.' "

That led Sweet to a meandering walk through history.

- The world's a better place because a German monk named Martin Luther didn't say, "I don't do doors."
- The world's a better place because an Oxford don named John Wesley didn't say, "I don't do preaching in fields."
- The world's a better place because
    Moses didn't say, "I don't do mass migrations."
    Noah didn't say, "I don't do arks."
    Rahab didn't say, "I don't do spies."
    Ruth didn't say, "I don't do mothers-in-law."
- The world's a better place because
    David didn't say, "I don't do giants."
    Peter didn't say, "I don't do gentiles."
    Paul didn't say, "I don't do prisons or shipwrecks."
- The world's a better place because
    Joseph didn't say, "I don't do adoptions."
    Mary didn't say, "I don't do virgin births."
- The world's a better place because Jesus Christ, the Lord of glory didn't say, "I don't do crosses."[5]

And your world and your marriage will be a better place if you don't say, "I don't do _____."

6

Dare to Share

A WOMAN WHO HAD SAILED TO EUROPE with a friend phoned her husband when she arrived in London. Things had been rather strained when she left, but they exchanged pleasantries and routine information. Then she asked, "How's Fifi?" Her beautiful Persian cat was very special to her, and she knew her husband was more than a little jealous of the affection she lavished upon her pet. But she was totally unprepared for his curt reply: "The cat's dead." She let out a scream and abruptly hung up the phone. For two days, she was inconsolable.

Finally she regained enough composure to telephone and to confront her husband. She began to berate him for his carelessness with her pet. More sensitive by now, he carefully explained that the cat had suddenly contracted a strange illness and the veterinarian had been unable to help. When he told her how much he had spent trying to save her cat, she began to realize that he had done his best.

Then the battle lines shifted. "The way you told me was cruel and sadistic. You were totally insensitive." "I'm sorry. What should

I have done?" "You could at least have broken the news gradually. When I called you from here, you could have told me the cat was on the roof. Then, when I called from Paris, you could have told me it had fallen and been hurt. Then, when I got to Rome, you could have said the doctors were concerned but hopeful. And then maybe by Athens I would have been ready for the news. You need to work on your sensitivity." "I'll try. I'll really try." "O.K. By the way, have you heard from my sister?" "Well, dear, she's playing on the roof."

Almost inevitably, when researchers study the main causes of marital breakdown, communication emerges as the prime culprit. That is striking because when I ask couples in premarital counseling why they are getting married, almost always the response is about communication. "We just feel so comfortable sharing everything together. I've never had anybody I feel so open with." But when troubled couples come in for counseling, their complaint is, "We don't talk anymore," or "we can't talk about anything without fighting," or "I just don't know him anymore."

Covenant commitment is the glue of marriage. But a lasting marriage is not necessarily a good or healthy marriage. Couples sometimes stay together because it's "the deal" or because of social pressure, emotional dependency, financial necessity, lethargy, or some other reason. A relationship that is healthy and mutually satisfying requires not only the glue of commitment but also the oil of communication. Communication keeps a marriage flexible and responsive, and allows couples to live in harmony rather than discord. I want to be understood; I want to be accepted; I want to be taken seriously; I want to understand—the key to all these is communication.

The most comprehensive biblical passage on communication is found in Ephesians 4:25–5:2. Three themes intersect in Paul's words which will set the agenda for our next four chapters:

Therefore each of you must put off falsehood and speak truthfully to his neighbor, for we are all members of one body. "In your anger do not sin: Do not let the sun go

*down while you are still angry, and do not give the devil a
foothold. He who has been stealing must steal no longer,
but must work, doing something useful with his own hands,
that he may have something to share with those in need.*

*Do not let any unwholesome talk come out of your
mouths, but only what is helpful for building others up
according to their needs, that it may benefit those who
listen. And do not grieve the Holy Spirit of God, with
whom you were sealed for the day of redemption. Get rid
of all bitterness, rage and anger, brawling and slander,
along with every form of malice. Be kind and
compassionate to one another, forgiving each other, just as
in Christ God forgave you.*

*Be imitators of God, therefore, as dearly loved
children and live a life of love, just as Christ loved us and
gave himself up for us as a fragrant offering and sacrifice
to God.*

In this chapter we want to look at the positive side of the
communication process. Communication clearly involves the
exchange of information. But effective communication involves
more than this. It occurs when what I think and feel about
something is transferred to another person, so that he or she
engages my emotions as well as my ideas. Communication occurs
when I understand not only what my wife thinks but also what she
feels. That alone will not solve our problems, but they cannot truly
be solved without this as the basis. In this passage, Paul establishes
three principles that undergird effective communication.

Before considering those three principles, we need to recognize
Paul's overriding assumption. The great theme of Ephesians 4 is
the Spirit-created unity of God's people. The unity of the Spirit is
God's act, in Christ, which binds the church as one. If this is true of
all believers, it is especially true of two Christ followers who are
united not only in faith but also in marriage. The command is all
the more emphatic: "Make every effort to keep [guard and protect]
the unity of the Spirit through the bond of peace" (Ephesians 4:3).
Christ followers should have a passion for unity that motivates
their communication with one another.

EFFECTIVE COMMUNICATION REQUIRES LOVING HONESTY

"Therefore," Paul exhorts, "each of you must put off falsehood and speak truthfully to his neighbor, for we are all members of one body." On the most basic level, this prohibits lying, words of deception. Lies are the termites of trust. They eat the heart out of a relationship, and under pressure, it will collapse. In my counseling as a pastor, I have learned to put up with a lot of things. But it is almost impossible to help or to stay willing to help a person who persistently lies. When deception and falsehoods become a pattern, all hope for a meaningful relationship vanishes.

Falsehood, however, involves more than words of deception. Paul's word "put off" is the term used for disrobing, for taking off clothes. We speak of masks, and a fundamental truth is that masks of deception block true communication. As we saw in chapter 3, one of the first effects of sin was fig leaves, Adam and Eve hiding from one another, covering their shame, fears, and weaknesses. Masks and fig leaves hide who we are. As Robert Louis Stevenson put it:

> Here we are, most of us sitting at the window of our heart, crying for someone to come in and love us. But then we cover up the window with the stained glass of pride or anger or self-pity, so that no one can glimpse the lonely self inside.

Masks cannot communicate. As long as I am hiding, you can see only the surface, never the heart. There is safety behind the mask—no one can see the real self. But there is loneliness as well. Bruce Larson reproduces a letter he received from a woman whose husband was obviously gifted at living behind a mask:

> My husband is a much-beloved church leader, praised and admired. Doctors tell me he is psychotic, a very sick man. When you see the one you love so much turning bitterly hostile, drawing further and further away in a shell of loneliness, yet still teaching all the truth, there is a continuing grief that cannot be expressed.

Every attempt at help is blocked. Every expression of love is interpreted in the wrong way. *And all the while his Christian friends admire and praise him and force him further and further into his prison of loneliness, where any admission of fault or failure becomes so threatening that it seems to mean destruction* [emphasis added].[1]

There is more to Paul's words than putting off falsehood. He calls us to "speak truthfully," to be truthful. Just as falsehood is more than words of deception, truthfulness is more than honesty. It is integrity, consistency, authenticity, vulnerability. Nor is Paul merely calling us to blurt out blunt words, with the excuse, "Well, it's true." I've met some people who claim to be honest who are merely cruel. That is why Paul calls us in verse 15 to "speak the truth in love." Honesty without love is selfishness.

I sin with my tongue far more often than I care to admit. But at my best, I try to ask myself whether telling Elizabeth the "truth" will help her or harm her. Suppose I were to decide that I didn't like her dimples (that is a very safe illustration—I love them!). To tell her that might be honest. It would not be loving, especially since she can do nothing about them. That makes it my problem, not hers, and my need is to go to God to ask Him to change my heart. Speaking the truth doesn't mean blurting out whatever sinful thought arises in my mind.

Loving honesty calls me to recognize honestly the problems that are present in our relationship or in my behavior, and to speak about them clearly. Loving honesty calls me to admit truthfully my needs and to express my feelings with integrity. It challenges me to share myself honestly with my partner. There is a marvelous expression of how it feels to be locked out by loved ones in Paul's appeal to his Corinthian friends: "We have spoken freely to you Corinthians, and opened wide our hearts to you. We are not withholding our affection from you, but you are withholding yours from us. As a fair exchange—I speak as to my children—open wide your hearts also" (2 Corinthians 6:11–13).

In 1991, Elizabeth was diagnosed with breast cancer and required a modified radical mastectomy. It was the most searching, excruciating experience of our lives. All of a sudden, I was faced with the thought that I might lose her. I had always loved her body and found her physically alluring, and I'd wondered how I'd respond if a part of her that excited me was removed. Frankly, in the event, it was irrelevant. I needed and loved *her,* not her body parts, and it became a powerful time of deepening love.

But as she recovered from her surgery, it became evident that she didn't want me to see her. She felt mutilated, disfigured, and scarred. She knew I loved her, but would I really love her if I saw her as she really was? Of course I wished that her cancer was an illusion and surgery had been unnecessary, but I love *her* for all that she is. What cancer has taken from her is trivial compared to what Christ has given to her for me.

On a far deeper level, I am aware of my own longstanding sins and failures. Elizabeth has seen me as I really am, and she deeply loves me. She doesn't love everything about me, but she does love me. There is a wonderful security in that knowledge.

Perhaps the most common means of subverting quality communication in a marriage is the "engage-withdraw" syndrome. Most commonly, but certainly not exclusively, it is the wife who moves to engage her husband, to deepen the relationship, to confront an issue. That threatens her husband, for a variety of reasons and he withdraws, sometimes physically, often emotionally. The engager wants to confront the unpleasantness; the withdrawer feels overwhelmed and would rather deny it or internalize it. Engagers often become attackers and criticizers; withdrawers become stonewallers, short-circuiting any attempt to deal with the problem. This is a scenario played out countless times and is probably the most common pattern that brings couples to a counselor's office. It requires a bold commitment from both partners to learn to "putting off falsehood, speak the truth [in love]," to break through the engage-withdraw syndrome.

EFFECTIVE COMMUNICATION RESPECTS THE POWER OF WORDS

My mother usually told me the truth, but she didn't when she tried to salve my feelings with the proverb, "Sticks and stones may break my bones, but names will never hurt me." I remember that she wasn't quite as philosophical when she heard me calling my brother names. All of a sudden, names were a big deal. Because "names" are a big deal. They wound more seriously, penetrate more deeply, and linger more permanently than sticks or stones. No wonder Solomon said, "The tongue has the power of life and death" (Proverbs 18:21). Our words matter. They expose the condition of our hearts and they determine the quality of our relationship.

It is easy to defend words said in the heat of the moment as excusable outbursts. "I didn't really mean it." Physical abuse is always wrong, always inexcusable, but verbal abuse is no less destructive. Sarcastic comments, put-downs, insults, names, criticisms, outbursts—these are verbal daggers that pierce to the heart.

> *He who guards his lips guards his life,*
> *but he who speaks rashly will come to ruin.*
> (Proverbs 13:3)

> *Reckless words pierce like a sword,*
> *but the tongue of the wise brings healing.*
> (Proverbs 12:18)

Paul's exhortation is, "Do not let any unwholesome talk come out of your mouths." The word *unwholesome* often describes what is decayed or rotten. It is used of overripe fruit and of rotting fish. To be unwholesome is not only to be useless (who wants to eat a rotten apple?) but contaminating ("one rotten apple spoils the barrel").

Paul doesn't define unwholesome speech, but it is easy to recognize the descending scale of "rottenness" we often follow:

1. *Complaints.* Every couple has them, usually focusing on the partner's actions. It is important to be able to voice our complaints and concerns. Valid complaints focus on actions, they are not attacks.

2. *Criticism.* We cross an important line when we move to words that attack the other person—blame, accusation, sarcasm, arguments, and insults. The issue is disrespect. Situation comedies

fill our minds with such speech, as couples engage in verbal battles designed to denigrate and belittle. But, in real life, harsh criticism is an attack on the other that wounds the heart.

3. *Contempt.* Words of contempt are intended to wound, to hurt, to destroy. Hostility and detachment put a marriage almost beyond the hope of recovery. The saddest marriages I have dealt with have been those where contempt was almost tangible, in bitter words, a contemptuous tone, and mocking body language.

Paul, however, does not merely leave us with the prohibition of unwholesome speech. He calls us to major on speech that ministers, nurtures, and encourages. Speak, he says, "only what is helpful for building others up according to their needs, that it may benefit [literally, give grace to] those who listen."

Four questions arise out of Paul's injunction to guide our speech.

1. *Is it helpful?*

Helpful words are good words that attack the problem but not the person. Good words show approval, give the benefit of the doubt, and focus on solutions, rather than blame.

It is helpful to recognize that, although men and women both use words, we don't necessarily use them in the same way. Deborah Tannen demonstrates in her insightful book *You Just Don't Understand* that men tend to use conversation to solve problems and make decisions. Women use conversation to work through ideas, to express feelings, and to establish rapport and intimacy.[2] But when a husband comes to a discussion "problem-solving" and a wife "feeling-sharing," the result is often unpleasant. The issue isn't that one approach is right and the other wrong. I just need to recognize that my words will be far more helpful if I understand what kind of conversation this is. Sometimes I want to "share feelings," and Elizabeth is almost always delighted. More often, she starts to share her feelings, I jump in to solve the problem (with some brilliantly insightful ideas, I must humbly say!) and she isn't very enthusiastic. Therefore, awareness of and sensitivity to our differences helps make my speech "helpful."

2. *Is it affirming and constructive?*

"Building others up" is Paul's concern. This is the language of affirmation and encouragement, of admiration and nurturance. Much of modern life tears us down and breaks us apart. A marriage needs to be a place of recharging one's emotional batteries and replenishing internal resources. I need to know that my partner is on my team.

There is another side of affirming, up-building speech, and that is shared laughter and good humor. There is a gentle bantering, a healing playfulness that makes our time together fun. I not only love my wife, I like her and enjoy her. We take our marriage very seriously and one way we do that is by not taking ourselves too seriously.

3. *Is it timely?*

Learning to speak "according to their needs" means learning to listen. One of the primary acts of love is to listen, to pay attention. Too often we talk past one another, hardly aware of the currents running deep in our partner's heart. Emotional distance is nearly always the product of drifting, not disaster.

> *A fool finds no pleasure in understanding*
> *but delights in airing his own opinions. . . .*
> *He who answers before listening—*
> *that is his folly and shame.*
> (Proverbs 18:2, 13)

David Augsburger notes that "to listen is the queen of compliments; to ignore the chief of insults. . . . Love is a warm listener."[3] But I have needed to learn that listening isn't merely hearing the words. It is hearing the person. I am good at doing two things at a time—reading and watching television, talking with Elizabeth and reading the paper. And when she asks, "Did you hear what I said?" I can usually repeat it word for word. The problem is that she doesn't feel listened to because I haven't properly given her my attention. "The first act of love is to listen," a wise person once said.

4. *Is it gracious?*

"So that it may benefit [give grace to] those who hear." Grace gives what is needed, not what is deserved. Grace looks beyond faults to minister to needs. Grace makes the other feel valued and accepted. Grace appreciates the significance of the other's problems, plans, and dreams. Grace enables someone to say what Eliphaz said of Job,

> *Your words have supported those who stumbled;*
> *you have strengthened faltering knees.*
> (Job 4:4)

EFFECTIVE COMMUNICATION REQUIRES CLEAR BOUNDARIES

Imagine a cliff that falls off into the ocean. Wise people will avoid the edge of the cliff, and loving parents with small children will make sure that they are kept at a safe distance. But if a proper fence is placed on the edge, the situation changes. Danger is not removed but the structure provides a new security. Good fences are not hostile barriers; they are protective limits. They give freedom.

Good communication needs clear boundaries. No normal people can live in a relationship as complex and challenging as marriage without arousing strong feelings and revealing deep differences. There must be clear boundaries in which strong feelings can be expressed, but there must also be a deeply shared conviction that some things must not be tolerated. Some things once said cannot be unsaid; some things once done cannot be undone. It is one thing to fight, it is another to fight dirty.

Paul describes communicable disorders, things that are out of bounds. "Get rid of" is strong language. It describes the emphatic rejection of behaviors and attitudes that breach security. There are three major concerns of Paul:

Bitterness—anger turned inward, that poisons the spirit and turns life and relationships sour

Temper—Paul speaks of rage (not anger), hostility, brawling (a term that describes shouting and clamor), and slander (insults). The issue of conflict is the subject of the next chapter, but Paul clearly views these as forms of destructive conflict.

Malice—the cold anger that wants nothing good for the other, the retreat into silence, coldness, and alienation.

As always, Paul balances the negative with the positive: "Be kind and compassionate to one another, forgiving each other just as in Christ God forgave you." Forgiveness will be the subject of chapter 9. It is an indispensable characteristic of a healthy marriage. Kindness is the commitment to do what is useful, and to do it with sensitivity and without severity. Compassion represents a fascinating Greek word, one that literally means "to have good inner organs." It is commitment to stay soft and sensitive, to deal with creeping separateness, to remove relational scar tissue.

This is not an automatic process. It takes work to stay kind and compassionate. Life has a way of hardening us. Time has a way of desensitizing us. Duties have a way of distracting us. All too easily couples who once rejoiced in their intimacy can become emotional strangers. It is not enough to establish rules and fences that describe what is out of bounds. A couple must plan to live a life of love; they must practice deeds of kindness and compassion. This requires a consistent investment of healthy communication, not just emergency measures of rescue.

Time with your partner is an investment, not an expense. When we couldn't afford anything more, Elizabeth and I made sure we went out every week for breakfast. We were investing in undistracted time with one another. (After two weddings within a year and three college educations, we're back to breakfasts.) Even now, in the empty-nest stage, we need to plan time together. We need to work to stay connected.

Communication isn't really very difficult. By that I mean that the principles are pretty simple and rather obvious. On the other hand, communication is difficult and demanding. It demands of me what I do not always feel like giving. But the alternative is loneliness, and no loneliness is more painful than the loneliness of an empty marriage.

7

The Porcupine Process

S AMUEL WESLEY WAS NOT an easy man to live with. Strict and impatient, he became unpopular enough with his parishioners that some of them set fire to his house three times to encourage him to relocate. His wife Susanna was almost equally strong-minded and stubborn. She needed to be to raise the nineteen children she bore, and to cope with her husband's prickly personality.

Sparks flew when Samuel and Susanna collided. They battled over many things, especially politics. England was in a tumultuous time with rival claimants to the throne. Samuel was a fervent follower of the new king, William of Orange, while Susanna was loyal to the Stuart dynasty, and the exiled James II. One night, when Samuel prayed for King William, Susanna refused to add her "Amen." Samuel exploded. Falling on his knees, he asked the Lord to judge him for his sin if he touched his wife before she repented of her sin. Then he stood to his feet, looked her in the eyes, and said, "We must part, for if we have two kings we must have two beds!" So he strode out of the house, mounted his horse, and rode off into a year's separation.

Fortunately for the Wesleys, King William died, and the two felt free to reunite in 1702. Within a year, as a visible product of their reconciliation, John was born. John Wesley went on to become one of history's great preachers, the human agent of the great Methodist revival that transformed England and deeply affected the thirteen colonies. His younger brother Charles became one of the church's most prolific hymnwriters.

John's genius didn't extend to marriage. He married unwisely and experienced a very tumultuous home life. Friends on one occasion entered the home to find Wesley's wife dragging her husband around the room by his hair! When she finally left, he wrote in his journal, "I have not left her; I would not send her away; I will not recall her."

I find it hard not to smile when I read of the Wesleys' troubles. But I'm sure that they didn't find it at all humorous. There are no conflict-free marriages. The effect of sin makes that impossible. Nor would it be desirable. Just as there is turbulence where two rivers come together, there will be turbulence when two lives together make something new. But the turbulent convergence produces a river of much greater power. If they are truly to come together, a husband and wife must work hard to integrate their differences and blend their strengths. But conflict, wrongly handled, can tear apart the fabric of a marriage.

Someone has compared marriage to two porcupines trying to survive an Arctic winter. When the mercury drops and the snow begins to fly, they cuddle together for warmth. But when they do their quills stick one another. So they pull apart, but soon begin to shiver. So they move together again—and stick each other. And so the dance goes on—damaging and distancing, damaging and distancing, until they realize that if they don't learn to adjust to one another, they will never survive.

One of the facts of marriage is that we both have quills— feelings, attitudes, behaviors, and ideas that really can stick our partner. Learning to make our differences work for us rather than against us is one of the fundamental necessities of marriage. A healthy marriage is adjusted to reality. Productive conflict deepens a relationship, but destructive conflict threatens it. We all recognize that unmanaged conflict can have devastating effects. We're not always clear what such conflict looks like, but there is a biblical event that provides a case study in conflict gone wrong. The passage has nothing directly to do with marriage but the process which led to the outbreak of a tragic civil war in ancient Israel, an event that permanently divided the nation, is instructive in avoiding marital warfare.

HOW TO START A CIVIL WAR: DESTRUCTIVE CONFLICT

Rehoboam went to Shechem, for all the Israelites had gone there to make him king. When Jeroboam son of Nebat heard this (he was still in Egypt, where he had fled from King Solomon), he returned from Egypt. So they sent for Jeroboam, and he and the whole assembly of Israel went to Rehoboam and said to him: "Your father put a heavy yoke on us, but now lighten the harsh labor and the heavy yoke he put on us, and we will serve you."

Rehoboam answered, "Go away for three days and then come back to me." So the people went away.

Then King Rehoboam consulted the elders who had served his father Solomon during his lifetime. "How would you advise me to answer these people?" he asked.

They replied, "If today you will be a servant to these people and serve them and give them a favorable answer, they will always be your servants."

But Rehoboam rejected the advice the elders gave him and consulted the young men who had grown up with him and were serving him. He asked them, "What is your advice? How should we answer these people who say to me, 'Lighten the yoke your father put on us'?"

The young men who had grown up with him replied, "Tell these people who have said to you, 'Your father put a heavy yoke on us, but make our yoke lighter'—tell them, 'My little finger is thicker than my father's waist. My father laid on you a heavy yoke; I will make it even heavier. My father scourged you with whips; I will scourge you with scorpions.'"

Three days later Jeroboam and all the people returned to Rehoboam, as the king has said, "Come back to me in three days."

The king answered the people harshly. Rejecting the advice given him by the elders, he followed the advice of the young men and said, "My father made your yoke heavy; I will make it even heavier. My father scourged you with whips; I will scourge you with scorpions." So the king did not listen to the people, for this turn of events was from the LORD, *to fulfill the word the* LORD *had spoken to Jeroboam son of Nebat through Ahijah the Shilonite.*

When all Israel saw that the king refused to listen to them, they answered the king:

> "What share do we have in David,
>   what part in Jesse's son?
> To your tents, O Israel!
>   Look after your own house, O David!"

So the Israelites went home. But as for the Israelites who were living in the town of Judah, Rehoboam still ruled over them.

King Rehoboam sent out Adoniram, who was in charge of forced labor, but all Israel stoned him to death. King Rehoboam, however, managed to get into his chariot and escape to Jerusalem. So Israel has been in rebellion against the house of David to this day.

When all the Israelites heard that Jeroboam had returned, they sent and called him to the assembly and made him king over all Israel. Only the tribe of Judah remained loyal to the house of David.
(1 Kings 12:1–20)

All wars are sad but civil wars are the saddest of all. I remember the somberness that still seems to hang over the battlefield memorial at Gettysburg. To envision men who had schooled together and worked together killing one another is heartbreaking. All conflicts are sad, but marital conflicts are the saddest of all, and often the most violent. To look at wedding pictures, and then years later, to hear the angry words, to feel the intense animosity, and to watch the destructive behaviors is tragic. Conflict may be inevitable, but destructive conflict is the product of violating some very specific principles.

The book of Proverbs is addressed from a father (Solomon) to his son. Rehoboam was Solomon's oldest son, the heir to Israel's throne, and he had heard his father's words. But he hadn't listened. It really doesn't matter how wise the counsel you receive is if you don't follow it!

> *Better a patient man than a warrior,*
> *a man who controls his temper than one who*
> *conquers a city.*
> (Proverbs 16:32)

> *Starting a quarrel is like breaching a dam;*
> *so drop the matter before a dispute breaks out.*
> (Proverbs 17:14)

The incident in 1 Kings 12 does not emerge out of nowhere. All conflicts have roots. Rehoboam became the king of Israel after the glorious reign of his father, Solomon. There was a festering sore in the nation, one that had never been fully resolved. There were hostilities between the tribes that went back to the time of Saul and David. Much of it was petty jealousy, some of it was justified, but ten tribes (Judah and Benjamin were the exceptions) felt marginalized. As well, Solomon had left some unfinished business. He had levied high taxes and required forced labor so that the people felt oppressed. Rehoboam also had some inner conflicts and inner doubts which he brought to the throne with him. Following a great man like Solomon was no small challenge, under the best of circumstances. But the pressure on Rehoboam only exposed his deep inner flaws.

The issues confronting Rehoboam as he became king were significant but they were not insolvable. It is not unlike many marriages. The people of Israel were troubled but they were not unreachable: "Your father put a heavy yoke on us, but now lighten the harsh labor and the heavy yoke he put on us, and we will serve you." Rehoboam had a tremendous opportunity to consolidate his position. Conflict is an opportunity to grow and strengthen a relationship. But Rehoboam not only fails to seize his opportunity, he destroys his nation. Why?

The first mistake is that he *focused on himself.* Rehoboam consulted the elders but he did not turn to God to seek wisdom. He is totally focused on being a winner, on what is best for him. The people are to be used for his purposes. His concern is "what's best for me?" not "what's best for God's people?" He is self-centered rather than servant-minded.

If I enter a conflict concerned only with winning and protecting my turf, I will inevitably alienate the other and destroy trust. A self-focused mind-set poisons any relationship. "If I don't get my way, you won't get yours." An adversarial attitude may work well in the courtroom or on the football field. It kills marriages.

Second, Rehoboam *refused to listen.* He consults the experienced leaders from his father's reign, but when they give an answer he doesn't like, he turns to his inexperienced peers. Rehoboam has no interest in truth or wisdom. He merely canvasses opinions to confirm his prejudices. He stubbornly turns a deaf ear to contrary opinion.

> *A fool finds no pleasure in understanding,*
> *but delights in airing his own opinions.*
> (Proverbs 18:2)

> *He who answers before listening—*
> *that is his folly and his shame.*
> (Proverbs 18:13)

People come to counselors and pastors with that attitude. "Tell me what I want to hear and tell them what they need to hear." An unteachable attitude breeds an unreachable heart which produces unsolvable problems. According to John Gottman, "Stonewalling is the most destructive of the [risk factors] leading to a marriage's downfall."[1]

Third, he *rejected compromise and negotiation.* Rehoboam could only think win-lose, not win-win. For him, life was an all-or-nothing, win-at-any-price business. There are other destructive options. The lose-win mind-set is so fearful of conflict that it immediately capitulates and surrenders. This buys a temporary peace at the cost of personal integrity and a righteous resolution of the problem. Others think lose-lose: "I may lose but you're going to lose as well." The story is told of a man who saw an advertisement that read, "Mercedes, $100." Although he was convinced it must be a misprint or a come-on, he decided it was worth a try. Amazingly, he discovered the car was virtually brand new and in excellent condition. He quickly paid the money and asked the woman why she was selling the car for so little: "My husband just ran off with his secretary. He told me to sell his car and send him the money, so I'm doing it." Classic lose-lose.

Wise people think win-win. They want to maximize the benefits for anyone. At an early stage in my marriage, when I was in a vigorous win-lose mind-set in a discussion with Elizabeth, I suddenly realized that I could win this fight but lose everything I wanted in my marriage. All of a sudden, my being right was far less important than my marriage being right. Compromise, unless it costs my integrity, is a sign of wisdom, not weakness.

Fourth, Rehoboam *chose inflammatory language.* "My little finger is thicker than my father's waist [probably "male organ," a crude male joke]. My father laid on you a heavy yoke; I will make it heavier. My father scourged you with whips; I will scourge you with scorpions." His words were blowtorch words, designed to burn and inflame. I remember reading a description of David Lloyd-George, the English political leader of the World War I era: "When angry, he became a fierce opponent, capable of cruel words and ruthless actions: 'I wound where I can hurt most.' "

I suspect that Rehoboam's tone was consistent with his words—full of contempt and macho swagger. "He answered the people harshly." His cruel tone was clearly as insulting as his hard words. Rather than respecting old tribal wounds, Rehoboam aggressively rubs salt into those wounds. "The tongue also is a fire, a world of evil among the parts of the body. It corrupts the whole person, sets the whole course of his life on fire, and is itself set on fire by hell" (James 3:6). Rehoboam epitomizes the truth of those words.

Fifth, he *exploited his position*. Rehoboam plays his trump card. He is the king and things will be done his way. Rather than fixing the problem, he forces his solution. He used power rather than persuasion. We are not told, but I suspect that Rehoboam's power play had far more to do with inner weakness than true strength. He is defensive, insecure, and posturing. It was easier to escalate hostility than to listen sensitively.

"When all Israel saw that the king refused to listen," the text says. Destructive conflict breeds division. Rehoboam got his way but he lost his nation. A civil war results, which led to the permanent division of Israel and Judah. He won, but he and his people paid a terrible price.

> *An offended brother is more unyielding than a fortified city,*
> *and disputes are like the barred gates of a citadel.*
> (Proverbs 18:19)

We can choose to handle conflict destructively; we cannot choose the results.

It is important to recognize that the conflict itself was not in Rehoboam's control. The fact of conflict was inherited from his father; the form the conflict took was entirely within his control. In marriage, we need to acknowledge our differences. Conflict is inevitable. We are not the same. We need to recognize the opportunity conflict provides to bring about a new level of mutual understanding and intimacy. Most of all, we need to resolve our differences in a win-win manner. It ultimately matters less what the conflict is about than the way it is handled.

HOW TO FIGHT FAIRLY: CONSTRUCTIVE CONFLICT

> *"In your anger do not sin": Do not let the sun go*
> *down while you are still angry, and do not give the devil a*
> *foothold.* (Ephesians 4:26–27)

In contrast to Rehoboam's negative model, we need to listen carefully to Paul's Spirit-led instructions. He begins by quoting

Psalm 4:4, "In your anger do not sin." There is a wealth of meaning in that simple phrase. Conflict is inevitable—because we are sinful and self-centered, because we are different, and because we are changing. The first truth of a Christian home is that sinners live there. Two sinners united in marriage cannot make a sinless marriage. But conflict is not always due to sin. We differ as men and women. We differ in our personalities and temperaments. We differ in our life experiences, our personal agendas, and our expectations.

If conflict is inevitable, it is also revealing. What we get upset about tells an enormous amount about us as individuals and as a couple. When trivial issues become major sources of conflict, that reveals a marriage in serious trouble.

Conflict is also important. Healthy conflict isn't quarreling. There are clear and strong warnings about quarreling in Scripture:

> *Starting a quarrel is like breaching a dam;*
> *so drop the matter before a dispute breaks out.*
> (Proverbs 17:14)

> *He who loves a quarrel loves sin.*
> (Proverbs 17:19)

> *It is to a man's honor to avoid strife,*
> *but every fool is quick to quarrel.*
> (Proverbs 20:3)

Conflict is an opportunity to reach a new depth of relationship. Experts on conflict management have concluded that people who constantly withdraw from conflict shrink the circle of their experiences and relationships. When too many areas of our lives are "out of bounds," we end up with very little common ground. At the same time, conflict operates like a warning light on a dashboard. It tells me where attention is needed to prevent serious damage.

John Gottman, a professor of psychology at the University of Washington, has done an extended study of two thousand married couples over twenty years to discover the factors that bind a marriage together or tear it apart. His conclusion, in his book *Why Marriages Succeed or Fail,* isn't, in itself, very remarkable: "A lasting marriage results from a couple's ability to resolve the conflicts that are inevitable in any relationship."[2] What is striking is his further observation. He reports that couples deal with conflict using various patterns—avoiding, validating, and volatile. He observes that the style of problem solving is far less important than the context of problem facing: "As long as there is five times as much positive feeling and interaction between husband and wife as there is negative, we found the marriage was likely to be stable."[3] The basic tone of a relationship is absolutely crucial.

David Myers reports a similar discovery in his insightful book *The Pursuit of Happiness.* Couples were asked to monitor their arguments and their sexual relationship. Almost every couple that engaged in sex more often than they argued described themselves as happily married. Conversely, no couple that argued more than they had sexual intercourse rated themselves as happy.[4] It is tempting to read this simply as an affirmation of sexual frequency. Enjoyable as that may be, it is more likely that frequent sexual contact is a product of marital enjoyment and harmony. Conflict does not destroy harmony, but there is a critical balance which must not be lost.

Conflict tiptoes on the borderline of sin. "In your anger do not sin." That is why *we need to choose our attitude carefully.* We can multiply evil instead of resolving differences. All too easily we can fall into attacking and retaliating.

We also need to *choose our goal wisely.* In contrast to Rehoboam, the goal is not to be right, but to get right with one another. The challenge is not to keep peace at all costs, but to build unity. True peace is not the absence of conflict so much as the presence of a deep underlying oneness.

Paul warns us that Satan is not a passive bystander. He is actively positioned to sow discord and disunity. "Do not give the devil a foothold" (Ephesians 4:27) reminds me that unresolved conflicts open a door to serious trouble. Years ago a young man came to me anxious about his marriage. I don't need to elaborate on the details but the flashpoint of conflict had become the toilet seat, and whether it was left up or down. The whole matter was complicated by the fact that they shared the bathroom with another couple. I suggested such wise things as getting an extra thick toilet seat cover when he finally said: "It's not really about the toilet seat. You see, when we fight, we just stop talking to each other for a few days. Then we begin again, but we never go back and talk about the problem. I feel like we've got a big closet that we throw all those things into, and if I open the door to throw in the toilet seat, everything else will fall out on me."

It was a picturesque way of stating an important fact. Unresolved conflicts don't vanish. They become free floating hostilities and frustrations, waiting for the next problem to emerge. And then, suddenly, trivial issues become prime irritants, because all the rest of the baggage is attached to it. The goal in conflict must not be just to keep peace but to establish a working harmony by resolving differences.

All of that means that, in conflict, we must choose our weapons carefully. These five "rules of engagement" are important as we work through the porcupine process.

1. *Attack the problem, not the person.*

The problem is *our* problem, not just your problem or my problem. It effects *us*. I've found it useful to think of the issue as in front of both of us, not between us. "We" are a nonnegotiable; "it" is the problem. So the issue needs to be heard carefully, described clearly, and attacked cooperatively. At the same time, no problem can be solved that is not owned and defined. The first step of healing is to identify the problem accurately and mutually.

2. *Fix the problem, not the blame.*

An amazing amount of energy is spent in times of conflict on blaming and excusing. The Lord Jesus calls me to focus on my own faults. Few passages are as relevant as Matthew 7:3–5:

> *"Why do you look at the speck of sawdust in your brother's eye and pay no attention to the plank in your own eye? How can you say to your brother, 'Let me take the*

speck out of your eye,' when all the time there is a plank in your own eye? You hypocrite, first take the plank out of your own eye, and then you will see clearly to remove the speck from your brother's eye."

Fixing the problem means that I will apologize readily for my contribution and that I will focus on solutions, not mistakes. The "ventilation" fad that encouraged people to focus on their feelings and vent their anger led to short-term relief and long-term regret. As Carol Travis notes in a careful study of anger, "People who are most prone to give vent to their rage get angrier, not less angry." [5]

3. *Keep it private, not public.*

There is a legitimate place for seeking wise, spiritual counsel. That is very different than enlisting allies among family and friends, a process that distorts friendship and betrays marital loyalty. When we draw others into the problem, the tendency is for a win-loss mind-set to develop, as others are encouraged to choose up sides.

4. *Do it now, not later.*

The injunction, "Do not let the sun go down while you are still angry," became one of the most important lessons of our first year of marriage. We determined before God not to go to bed angry with one another. We couldn't always solve the problem and we haven't always gotten to bed early, but we affirmed our commitment to "us" and sought to resolve the issue or defang it. But the issue is "who takes the first step?" God's answer is simple—you do, whether you have something against your partner (Matthew 18:15) or vice versa (Matthew 5:23–24). The recognition that unresolved conflicts become Satan's footholds means that *now* is the time.

5. *Pray it up when you bring it up.*

Conflict needs to be firmly placed in a context of love and prayer. "Above all, love each other deeply, because love covers over a multitude of sins." (1 Peter 4:8) It is virtually impossible to pray sincerely with your partner if conflict is unresolved between you. "Treat them with respect . . . so that nothing will hinder your prayers." (1 Peter 3:7)

The old saying is that nothing is as certain as death or taxes. Conflict in marriage is. But we can choose to fight to the bitter end or to a better end. The ability to resolve conflict is an essential ingredient of a healthy marriage. And when we deal with conflict we become like the old skin horse in Margery Williams' famous story of the Velveteen Rabbit:

> The Skin Horse had lived longer in the nursery than any of the others. He was so old that his brown coat was bald in patches and showed the seams underneath, and most of the hairs in his tail had been pulled out to string bead necklaces. He was wise, for he had seen a long succession of mechanical toys arrive to boast and swagger, and by-and-by break their mainsprings and pass away, and he knew that they were only toys, and would never turn into anything else . . . .
>
> "What is REAL?" asked the Rabbit one day, when they were lying side by side near the nursery fender, before Nana came to tidy the room. "Does it mean having things that buzz inside you and a stick-out handle?"
>
> "Real isn't how you are made," said the Skin Horse. "It's a thing that happens to you. When a child loves you for a long, long time, not just to play with, but REALLY loves you, then you become real."
>
> "Does it hurt?" asked the Rabbit.
>
> "Sometimes," said the Skin Horse, for he was always truthful.
>
> "When you are Real you don't mind being hurt."
>
> "Does it happen all at once, like being wound up," he asked, "or bit by bit?"
>
> "It doesn't happen all at once," said the Skin Horse. "You become. It takes a long time. That's why it doesn't often happen to people who break easily, or have sharp edges, or who have to be carefully kept. Generally, by the time you are Real, most of your hair has been loved off, and your eyes drop out and you get loose in the joints and very shabby. But these things don't matter at all, because once you are Real you can't be ugly, except to people who don't understand."[6]

8

Hazardous Waste

A FTER A LONG, HARD WINTER, the first signs of spring are greeted with great enthusiasm by people who live in the snowy north. April 26, 1986, was a beautiful spring day in the Ukraine, and one man went up on the roof to sun himself. Not long after, he returned to tell his wife that he had never seen anything like it—there was an unusual glow in the sky and his skin had turned brown in no time.

What he could not know was that his was a "nuclear tan." Within a few hours he was taken to the hospital with uncontrollable vomiting, and the rest of the story began to unfold. The closest town was a place called Chernobyl, and, at 1:23 A.M., nuclear reactor number four had begun to explode, spewing a deadly radioactive cloud equal to a thousand Hiroshimas.

The first response of government officials was *silence*. Local residents fishing in the cooling ponds of the reactor stood watching the fire, oblivious to the danger and unwarned. The second response was *denial*. Plant managers insisted that the reactor was intact, even while the nuclear cloud was spreading through huge areas of Europe. Stage three was *trivialization*. People in Kiev were told to close their windows and wash their hair, while recruits were sent into the disaster area uninformed and pathetically under-equipped. Trivialization soon became *cover-up*. Paper surgical masks were standard issue and, although radiation testing was done, it was done with the requirement that no one register more than 25 units. One veteran later observed, "You always tested at 24.8 or 24.9. No one ever seemed to go over 25." When some asked for Geiger counters, their request was ridiculed: "Why do you want to cause trouble? You don't need a Geiger counter. Everything is all right."

But they weren't all right. Radioactive disaster can't be wished away. Tens of thousands of deaths have resulted. It is estimated that one hundred thousand children have experienced birth defects, and the destructive effect upon vegetation and animal life is incalculable. And it is isn't over. Toxic waste remains, and scientists warn that the encasement around the reactor is disintegrating and more tragedies will follow.

Nuclear disasters are terrible things because they spread hazardous waste which kills slowly, cruelly, and certainly. Denial, trivialization, and cover-up only increase the danger. Hazardous waste does not go away on its own. It must be dealt with and properly disposed of.

When we enter into a marriage, we enter with high hopes and beautiful dreams. But we also bring into our marriage the fallout of the fall, the effects of sin. We have been contaminated by our own sins and the sins of others against us. Our sins build sinful habits, which do not vanish with our wedding vows. Other's sins cause painful hurts and learned, self-protective defenses. Marriage does not remove them. In fact the intimacy of marriage often serves to expose and sensitize some of the most private and painful areas of our lives. No wonder Carl Jung observed that marriage is the most complex of human relationships.

Sandra Wilson describes what she calls Wilson's law of relationships: *Hurt people hurt people.*[1] All of us have been hurt by life—with self-inflicted and other-inflicted wounds. The sad thing is that our response to those hurts often hurts those closest to us. A man, feeling rejected by his distant father, becomes a workaholic, ignoring his wife. A woman, abused by her father, becomes emotionally frigid but sexually promiscuous. Another, having been forced by her mother's alcoholism to become the caretaker for her siblings, becomes a pleaser and a perfectionist. A man, unable to handle the pressure of parental expectations, retreats into a fantasy world of pornography.

Many of our patterns will not be so self-evident but the equation holds. Hurt people hurt people, and unless we deal with those hurts in the presence of the Lord, they will become toxic waste, contaminating and endangering our most precious relationships.

There is a fascinating bit of insight given in standard pre-takeoff flight instructions. A flight attendant will tell us that, in the event of problems, oxygen masks will fall from their containers. "If you have a child, first put on your own mask, then your child's." I must confess that wouldn't be my first instinct. Care for my child, then myself. But I can be of no long-term help to my child if I'm incapacitated. There are times when properly looking after myself isn't selfishness, but servanthood. Healthy marriages require whole people, and if I am going to be a source of oxygen rather than a carrier of toxic waste, I need to allow the Lord to be moving me from a hurt person to a whole person.

The Lord proclaimed that His ministry was "to proclaim freedom for the prisoners and to release . . . the oppressed" (Luke 4:18). One of His most familiar statements describes this release:

> *At that time Jesus said, "I praise you, Father, Lord of heaven and earth, because you have hidden these things from the wise and learned, and revealed them to little children. Yes, Father, for this was your good pleasure.*
>
> *"All things have been committed to me by my Father. No one knows the Son except the Father, and no one knows the Father except the Son and those to whom the Son chooses to reveal him.*
>
> *"Come to me, all you who are weary and burdened, and I will give you rest. Take my yoke upon you and learn from me, for I am gentle and humble in heart, and you will find rest for your souls. For my yoke is easy and my burden is light."* (Matthew 11:25–30)

Sandra Wilson tells the story of a peasant living on the edge of starvation. One day he found a basket of fruit. Overcome by joy, he carried his treasure home, hiding it from anyone else. He lit a candle and sat down to his banquet. But when he took his first bite, he found it rotten and wormy. Tossing it aside, he picked up another piece of fruit. The same thing happened, and then once again. Torn between hunger and disgust he sat looking at the fourth piece of fruit, pondering his options. Then he leaned over, blew out the candle, and began to eat.[2]

It is sometimes tempting to make that choice—to blow out the light, live in the darkness, and cope with what life has given us. But the Lord gives another option—to turn on the light, see who we are, and respond wisely, not only to ourselves but to our God.

THE LORD'S DIAGNOSIS: THE PROBLEMS OF PEOPLE

The words we have quoted are among the best-known and most-loved of our Lord, because we find ourselves described: "Come to Me, all you who are weary and burdened, and I will give you rest."

According to Jesus, *people are weary*. The word means "to work to the point of exhaustion." There is a weariness of body, a physical exhaustion that comes from dealing with the demands of life. Few things impact a marriage as much as the hectic pace of life, and the incessant demands that especially effect a family with young children. There is also a weariness of heart, an emotional heaviness that often is the product of failure and guilt. The Lord Jesus saw people who were harassed and helpless (Matthew 9:36), He uses a term that describes a "thrown" sheep, a sheep that has gotten in a position where no matter how it struggled, it could not get back on its feet. Emotionally, we can reach the same place, where we feel stuck, unable to get away from where we are. There is also a weariness of spirit, an inner barrenness that comes from a misguided attempt to earn favor with God. We feel like competitors in a high jump competition. Every success only means that the level will be raised, and no matter how high we go, we're going to end up knocking the barrier down. God feels like an unpleasable parent, always demanding, always commanding, and never satisfied.

The Lord also tells us that *people are burdened*. We carry a burden of failure, times when we have fallen short of our own expectations or those of others. Some find themselves staggering under memories—things we have done wrong, or wrongs that have been done to us. Memories can haunt us, and load us down with shame, fear, and anger. We can also carry a load of habits, individual threads that have been woven into a heavy rope around our lives. I have been reminded time and again as I have counseled with couples and individuals of how many addictive patterns impact our marriages. Many battle with sexual addictions—enslavement to pornography, masturbation, lustful patterns, and sexual sin. Others carry chemical addictions, to alcohol or drugs, while others know the load of more socially acceptable addictions—to work, sports, television, ministry.

The Lord also indicates that *people are restless*. He offers "rest for your souls," because at the core of our being we often feel stirring, striving, and turmoil. We become distrustful of relationships, afraid to reveal our inner hungers, or we become consumers of relationships, hoping to find the person who will fill up the emptiness and calm our restlessness. It is easier to believe that the problem lies with my partner or my circumstances than with me. But the storm is more often internal, and we take it with us wherever we go or with whomever we are.

All of these things are effects of the fall and the source of toxic relationships. Wounds from the past, whether self-inflicted or other-inflicted, are a given. We cannot change them; we can overcome them. Our choice is to be controlled by them or to deal with them.

A rather corny story tells of some men who had flown into a remote lake in northern Canada for some hunting and fishing. On the day the trip ended, the float plane arrived and the men loaded in their gear and their trophies. The pilot told them they were overloaded: "We can't take off. We'll crash." "Sure you can. We've done it before. We'll give you an extra five thousand dollars." So the pilot revved the engines, barely lifted off the waters, then crashed back into the water. As they swam to shore, one hunter turned to another and said, "Well, we made it a thousand feet farther than last year."

Someone has observed that insanity is doing the same thing and expecting different results. People are weary, burdened, and restless. But if we do not deal with those realities, we are destined to bring the toxic waste of our past into our relationships.

THE LORD'S SOLUTION: THE PROBLEM OF THE PAST

The Lord Jesus offers relief to people like us. He frames it in terms of a prayer, a claim, and a promise. We need to recognize how important this is to the Lord. He saw His mission in terms of the manifesto He proclaimed in the synagogue in Nazareth:

> *"He has sent Me to proclaim freedom for the prisoners,*
> *and recovery of sight for the blind,*
> *to release the oppressed,*
> *to proclaim the year of the Lord's favor."* (Luke 4:18–19)

Long before recovery groups existed to help people walk steps to freedom, the Lord announced hope for the hopeless and release for the bound.

Relief is a secret the Lord reveals to the humble. There are, He says, two kinds of people: "the wise and the learned" and "little children." The Lord is not here speaking about age or intelligence, but about attitude of heart. The wise and learned are not characterized by intellectual prowess but by intellectual pride. They are the self-satisfied and self-content, who believe that they can resolve life's problems and mysteries by their own power. Little children are the very opposite. The Lord Jesus declared a fundamental life principle in Matthew 18:3–4: "Unless you change and become like little children, you will never enter the kingdom of heaven. Therefore, whoever humbles himself like this child is the greatest in the kingdom of heaven." Little children are the dependent and the humble, who declare their dependence on the Father.

The Lord blesses the humble who admit their need, the teachable who acknowledge their ignorance, the hurt who expose their wounds. One of the greatest things I can do for my marriage is to humble myself before the Lord and others, honestly admit my need, and seek help. Until I reach that point I will, like "the wise and the learned" of Jesus' day, go on in my self-deception, laying burdens on others they cannot bear. The words of 1 Peter state an unfailing principle that challenges me continually: "God opposes the proud but gives grace to the humble" (5:5). I don't want to meet God's resistance; I need His grace.

Some Indian tribes of South America have devised an ingenious monkey trap. They place a desired tidbit in a jar with a narrow neck and a wide bottom. The entrance is wide enough to allow the monkey's hand to enter but too narrow for it to withdraw a clenched fist. The secret to the trap's success is a monkey's nature. Very few monkeys are willing to release what they've grabbed, and so they are trapped by what they hold on to.

The same principle applies to people. What we hold, holds us. If we hold on to the past—its hurts, and habits—it holds us. We are, the twelve-step people tell us wisely, only as sick as our secrets. Relief is a gift the Lord gives to the humble, to those who declare their need and come for help.

Relief is a truth taught by God's Son. Embedded in the words of Jesus is one of the greatest claims ever to fall from His lips. It is important to recognize that deep truth is never an irrelevance. The more we understand of Christ, the more solidly we establish a foundation for our lives. Listen carefully to His words:

- "All things have been committed to Me by my Father." The Lord Jesus is the sovereign Lord, the all-powerful God, the authoritative Master. No problem is too much for Him; no circumstance is beyond His control.

- "No one knows the Son except the Father, and no one knows the Father except the Son." The Lord is claiming full equality with the Father. Only God the all-knowing can know God. The Lord Jesus knows all that the Father knows and knows as the Father knows. There are no limits of wisdom, no boundaries of understanding. The wisest human counselor is a mere novice compared to Him.

- "and those to whom the Son chooses to reveal Him." The Lord's mission is to bring us into an intimate relation with the triune God. "No one comes to the Father except through me" (John 14:6). "Whoever comes to me I will never drive away" (John 6:37). The Lord Jesus is not only authoritative and all-knowing, He is available and accessible, committed to revealing to us the Father's heart.

One of the greatest prophecies about the Lord Jesus is found in Isaiah 9:6,

> *For to us a child is born,*
> *to us a son is given,*
> *and the government will be on his shoulders.*
> *And he will be called*
> *Wonderful Counselor, Mighty God,*
> *Everlasting Father, Prince of Peace.*

There is a crucial connection between the first two names. There is a great blessing in finding a counselor who is biblically informed, personally wise, and practically skilled. I am very grateful for Christian counselors who possess important helping skills. They point us to the Wonderful Counselor who gives insight and direction. But human counselors, no matter how skilled, are limited. They can point out the path, encourage, and motivate, but they cannot internally empower. But the Lord Jesus is not only Wonderful Counselor, full of wisdom; He is Mighty God, full of power. He not only provides insight, He empowers transformation. It is God the Son who promises to help us deal with our toxic waste.

Relief is a gift given to believers. At the heart of the Lord's words is a promise of exchange: "Come unto me, all you who are weary and burdened, and I will give you rest." The invitation is to bring the burdens to the Lord, to let go of the baggage and the garbage, and to accept the gift of rest. We need to stop carrying and start resting. The Lord knows all there is to know about us, cares for us infinitely, graciously forgives us, and wisely empowers us.

But the gift of Christ's rest is only one part of the process. There is also the *gift of Christ's rule:* "Take my yoke upon you." A yoke is a bar or frame that farmers used to link two animals together so that they could work together. The Lord, as a carpenter, would have made many yokes. In the ancient work, they were not factory-made, but custom-made to fit the animal comfortably and maximize his energy.

Usually the yoke is a symbol of bondage in the Bible. For example Paul describes legalism as "a yoke of slavery" (Galatians 5:1). It is not hard to see why. To be yoked "unequally" puts a terrible pressure on an animal. To be tied to a hurtful, destructive partner, to carry the yoke of unrealistic expectations, to wear a heavy yoke of bondage to the past, enslaves. But the paradox of Christ's yoke is that what might seem to bind us in fact sets us free. The yoke of Christ represents His authority, His rule. And that rule brings freedom. To change the picture, a kite is bound to earth by the string, but the string is what sets it free to fly. Cut the string and it cannot soar.

The "rest" of Christ is found only in the "rule" of Christ. To stretch the image, His purpose is to plow something with our lives. His goal is not merely to give us rest but to give us purpose; not just to ease our pain but to accomplish His plan. The yoke of Christ means replacing hurtful habits with holy habits, and the synergy of being in harness with Him means that we can accomplish far more than we could ever imagine.

I don't want to leave this all sounding so theoretical. We began the chapter with the image of toxic waste and end it with a very different picture of plowing a field. The central point is that we all carry burdens; we all wear a yoke. The past is a very present creature in our marriages. Our hurts, our hopes, our reactions, our expectations are all shaped by the issues of our past. If those are not recognized, owned, and dealt with, we will drag the past like chains into our marriage. We cannot remove the past but we can, by God's grace, arrest its legacy so that it does not contaminate the future, in our marriage or in our children.

But good intentions are not enough. I need to choose: "Take my yoke upon you." Choosing the yoke of Christ means owning my weariness, my burdens, and my soul restlessness and humbly coming to Jesus. It means not only accepting His rest but yielding to His rule, as He gently but firmly begins to plow His purposes in my life. "I am this way because of my past" must give way to "I'm becoming this way because of Jesus." "And learn from me" calls me to relearn my way of thinking, to reframe my view of reality, to renew my patterns of behavior with the Lord Jesus as my model. His yoke is never abusive, "for I am gentle and humble in heart . . . my yoke is easy and my burden is light."

When the Lord speaks in Matthew, His invitation is for individuals and His call is for a very personal relationship with Him. The rest of the New Testament eloquently reveals that people become the Lord's agents in helping us to deal with the toxic waste and to learn of Jesus. The wise encouragement of a godly leader, the insightful counsel of a biblically informed counselor, the mutual support of a recovery group, the spiritual encouragement of an accountability group, and above all, the loving, sensitive interaction of a marriage partner can become the Lord's agents of helping us take up His yoke, to learn of Him, and to find His rest for our souls. One of the greatest gifts I can give to my spouse and children is courageously and deliberately to acknowledge my "toxic waste," to bring it to the cross, and to trust and cooperate with the Lord's transforming power. And that inevitably means facing head-on the issue of forgiveness.

9

The Freedom of Forgiveness

W HEN I WAS A HIGH SCHOOL STUDENT, I went to prison for the first time. That was more than thirty years ago, but in my memory, I can still hear clanging cell doors and echoing footsteps in those concrete corridors, I can taste the clammy fear that rose in my throat. As the group of us filed through the federal penitentiary, doors slammed shut behind us and we passed numerous control points. Occasionally we would enter courtyard areas where we could see three floors of cells. I've never forgotten the sight of men locked into tiny rooms, lacking privacy or dignity. It doesn't take much effort to recall the almost tangible mood of rage and violence, of anger and sadness, of waste and despair, that emanated from those men. The jeers and insults many prisoners directed at our singing group only intensified the effect. Still, I was glad to be part of a group with a message of true spiritual freedom in a place like that.

Prisons are a tragic necessity in a fallen world. There is however another kind of imprisonment almost as sad but far more subtle. It is a prison of the spirit—a jail without physical bars. Many remain locked inside a dungeon of bitterness, held captive by

111

an unforgiving, unyielding spirit. Two people cannot live in a relationship like marriage without sinning and being sinned against. How we deal with our own failures and those of our partner determines whether our relationship is an oasis or a jailhouse. Therefore, few issues in marriage are more important than forgiveness.

There are more lawyers than doctors in the United States. One cynic has suggested that this is because Americans are more interested in getting even than in getting better. That may not be the reason; but we all possess a desire to retaliate, to pay back, to teach someone a lesson. As my old rugby coach used to drill into us, "Don't get mad, get even." That philosophy led us into some pretty bruising battles, and some very exciting games. But what makes for good rugby doesn't make for good marriages. Revenge may be sweet, but it turns sour very fast! It devastates marriages, divides families, and destroys friendships.

The Lord Jesus obviously considered forgiveness to be a high priority issue, because He speaks of it continually. He came to bring us forgiveness; He also came to make us forgivers. "For if you forgive men when they sin against you, your heavenly Father will also forgive you. But if you do not forgive men their sins, your Father will not forgive your sins" (Matthew 6:14–15). The quality of our lives and the quality of our marriages is directly related to our ability to give and to receive forgiveness.

I find this all rather easy to say as I sit here writing in a quiet house with my nearest family members hundreds of miles away. C. S. Lewis put it well: "Forgiveness is a beautiful word until you have something to forgive." Forgiveness can be the hardest thing we ever do. Our forgiveness cost Jesus the cross. But forgiveness may become the most important thing we ever do to sustain or renew our marriage. Good marriages require good forgivers.

On the human level there is no greater example of forgiveness than Joseph and there is no more helpful picture of forgiveness in process than Genesis 45. It describes one of the most dramatic moments in the Old Testament, many years after the traumatic events that necessitated it. We want to turn to that ancient story for some very modern help.

FORGIVENESS IS A CHOICE WE MUST MAKE ABOUT THE PAST

If anyone was a prime candidate for bitterness, it was Joseph. Born into a highly dysfunctional family, he reaped the consequences of his father's foolish choices. Jacob had bred a polygamous, politicized family with children from four mothers. Joseph's own mother died while giving birth to Joseph's full brother, Benjamin. Deprived of the wife he loved most of all, Jacob lavished his love on Joseph. But this favoritism was a very mixed blessing. Joseph became the object of his brothers' scorn and hatred, the lightning rod for their sense of rejection. And when the opportunity came to hurt both Joseph and Jacob, the brothers took it with enthusiasm. Backing away from murder, they sold their seventeen-year-old brother to some passing traders, and he suddenly found himself a slave, without rights or status, in the land of Egypt.

The abuse didn't end there. Serving as a slave in the house of an Egyptian office, Joseph's abilities brought him to a position of responsibility. And Joseph's physical attributes brought him to the attention of his owner's wife. When he refused her seductions, she retaliated by accusing him of attempted rape. A slave had no hope of a fair trial in such circumstances, and Joseph was imprisoned. Even there, his abilities made him valuable, but once again he was forgotten and mistreated by people to whom he had done no wrong.

Virtually every person in Joseph's life had victimized him. His was a trail of experiences that often results in the dead end of bitterness, cynicism, and hopelessness. But that was not the outcome in Joseph's life. Despite such circumstances, the Lord was powerfully at work, and Joseph never succumbed to self-pity or despair. In a remarkable, God-superintended sequence of events, Joseph was elevated to become the second most powerful man in the nation. When an abused person who has not learned forgiveness reaches a position of power, he often will use that power as a weapon. Joseph never did. When we meet him in Genesis 45 he is about thirty-eight years of age, a man of absolute, unquestioned power. He could get revenge on whomever he desired. But he never used this position to retaliate against Potiphar, Potiphar's wife, or anyone else.

Bitter people share two things—an experience or a perceived experience of having been badly hurt, and a response of holding on to that hurt. Joseph had been deeply and undeniably sinned against, but *he had made a healing choice to let go of the past*. He was not untouched by the past—he bore the scars for his entire life—but he was uncrippled by it. We meet him in Scripture as a remarkably healthy man, a source of healing to everyone who encounters him.

Joseph had not merely let the past go, he had let it go *to God*. This is eloquently shown in a little note given to us in Genesis 41:50–52 :

> *Before the years of famine came, two sons were born to Joseph by Asenath daughter of Potiphera, priest of On. Joseph named his firstborn Manasseh and said, "It is because God has made me forget all my trouble and all my father's household." The second son he named Ephraim and said, "It is because God has made me fruitful in the land of my suffering."*

Names always had significance to the Hebrews, and that is especially true here. Manasseh means "made to forget," because "God has made me forget." Joseph chose to be controlled by his Lord, not by his brothers, or his father, and he made this choice long before he encountered his brothers later in life. Ephraim means "fruitful." The Lord had redeemed the past, and the place of suffering had become the source of blessing. Joseph is focused on the "fruit" of the past, not the peelings.

Joseph pushes us to the need to do business with God about those who have abused and sinned against us. Forgiveness is first and foremost a spiritual issue that brings me face to face with God. And in letting it go to Him, there is a freedom that produces fruitfulness. Ephraim ("fruitfulness") really does follow Manasseh ("forgetfulness"). My wife has illustrated this for me in a striking way. She has held several "burial services" with friends who have been deeply sinned against. They have taken a symbol of the person or sin and literally dug a hole and buried it, as a vivid event of letting it go to God.

During the Civil War Abraham Lincoln was under continual attack, from almost every side. The Confederates reviled him and disgruntled Unionists derided his every move. One friend began to lament the injustice of all this to Lincoln, who cut him short with the words, "Insane as it may be, I hold malice toward none of them. I have neither time or energy in this life to hold that kind of resentment." To fail to let the past go is to keep ghosts alive that haunt our present.

Joseph made another healing choice that sets the tables for Genesis 45. *He had chosen the tough love of restoration and reconciliation.* He made the choice not only to bury the past but to build a new future. When he first realized that his brothers had appeared in Egypt (in Genesis 42), he could have chosen to avoid them entirely and not to reopen an old wound. After all, he had a new life, a new family, a new home. He could have chosen to plaster over the differences, to live as if the past had never really happened, and to enjoy a superficial relationship with his family. He could also have chosen to exact revenge, to make them pay at compound interest, for their atrocious treatment of him. Instead, He chose reconciliation.

There is an important distinction between forgiveness and reconciliation. Forgiveness is a one-way street. It is something I choose before God. Reconciliation is a two-way street. It requires not only forgiveness but repentance on the part of the sinning party. It is the building of a new relationship, not simply the recovery of an old status. Forgiveness begins with the choice of a moment; reconciliation is the careful process of rebuilding. Reconciliation involves time because it requires trust, and trust grows.

Too often partners become unrealistic at this stage. I may forgive my partner's sins, but if that sin is part of a cyclical pattern of behavior, restoration is a very different question. A spouse who abuses and then remorsefully begs forgiveness; a partner who has a pattern of sexual infidelity; a mate whose addictive patterns lead to overwhelming remorse—how do we respond? Do we simply grant forgiveness and return to the status quo? The answer is no. Restoration without *demonstrated* repentance (which takes time) may only intensify the problem. The Lord commands us to keep forgiving (up to seventy times seven—Matthew 18:22). But the

New Testament also calls for church discipline, which insists on demonstrated change.

A story James Oliver Boswell tells helps me think through the process:

> Neither is the scriptural doctrine of forgiveness contrary to prudence. Some years ago I spoke on the subject of forgiveness in a certain prayer meeting. After my remarks, during the time of testimony, a carpenter arose with tears in his eyes and asked for advice. He had, some years previously, started to work on a scaffolding built by another carpenter. The scaffolding was poorly constructed and it gave way; and this Christian man was hospitalized for some weeks.
>
> "Now," said the Christian carpenter, "I do not feel bitterness in my heart toward that man and if I could do him good in any way I should certainly do so but," and at this the tears coursed down his face, "I cannot bring myself to step onto a scaffolding built by that man without first examining it and testing its security. I want to ask you Christian brethren if in your judgment I am cherishing unforgiveness?"
>
> Of course the unanimous answer was in the negative.[1]

I cannot overemphasize the importance of this. Restoration takes time, and trust is involved. Saying "I'm sorry" and "I forgive you" removes the damage but it doesn't rebuild the scaffold. We do need to test the scaffolding for a time. That's why Joseph does what he does in Genesis 42–44. He is not manipulating or deceiving. He is testing repentance. So when Judah, the spokesman for the brothers, the man who led his brothers to sell Joseph to slavery, offers to be Joseph's slave in Benjamin's place, lest Jacob be heartbroken, Joseph knows that a genuine transformation has taken place. True repentance has made restoration possible.

FORGIVENESS IS A BATTLE WE MUST FIGHT IN THE PRESENT

> *Then Joseph could no longer control himself before all his attendants, and he cried out, "Have everyone leave my*

presence!" So there was no one with Joseph when he made himself known to his brothers. And he wept so loudly that the Egyptians heard him, and Pharaoh's household heard about it.

Joseph said to his brothers, "I am Joseph! Is my father still living?" But his brothers were not able to answer him, because they were terrified at his presence.

Then Joseph said to his brothers, "Come close to me." When they had done so, he said, "I am your brother Joseph, the one you sold into Egypt! And now, do not be distressed and do not be angry with yourselves for selling me here, because it was to save lives that God sent me ahead of you. For two years now there has been famine in the land, and for the next five years there will not be plowing and reaping. But God sent me ahead of you to preserve for you a remnant on earth and to save your lives by a great deliverance.

"So then, it was not you who sent me here, but God. He made me father to Pharaoh, lord of his entire household and ruler of all Egypt. Now hurry back to my father and say to him, 'This is what your son Joseph says: God has made me lord of all Egypt. Come down to me; don't delay. You shall live in the region of Goshen and be near me—you, your children and grandchildren, your flocks and herds, and all you have. I will provide for you there, because five years of famine are still to come. Otherwise you and your household and all who belong to you will become destitute.' " (Genesis 45:1–11)

The emotions of this moment are overwhelming to consider, even four thousand years later. Joseph's instinct is for privacy—this is a moment so sacred no outsider can share it. And the feelings are overpowering. When his mask of aristocratic control slips away, Joseph's heart is revealed. Feelings that have been submerged for decades rush to the surface. Surging emotions that have been there since childhood now rush out, and the words terrify and astonish his brothers: "I am Joseph! Is my father still alive?"

It is often implied that forgiveness is natural and automatic, a transaction requiring little emotional capital. Nothing could be further from the truth. True forgiveness is hard and painful. It touches the deepest currents of our lives. It was painful for our Lord; painful for Joseph; and it will be painful for us. Nor is it a one-time event, done and finished once for all. Joseph was not lying when he named his son "Manasseh." God had made him "forget." But he had to choose to keep forgetting, especially now as he faces his brothers directly.

It is useful to step back and think about the nature of forgiveness. Forgiveness isn't overlooking a wrong ("forget it") or redefining the action ("you had a bad day"). To forgive isn't to minimize the offense ("it wasn't that big a deal"), nor is it reversing the wrong, by accepting the blame for another person's behavior ("I shouldn't have"). To forgive is not to excuse. We may tolerate weaknesses and understand mistakes, but we can only forgive sins. No one said it better than G. K. Chesterton: "Forgiveness is pardoning the unpardonable or it isn't forgiveness at all."

It has been very helpful for me to walk with Joseph down the path of forgiveness. There are, it seems, four steps.

First, *acknowledge the sin*. "I am your brother Joseph, the one you sold into Egypt." At a later time, when they raise the issue, he will be even more direct: "You intended to harm me" (50:20; or more directly, "You meant it for evil"). Joseph refuses to whitewash their crime by shifting responsibility ("I was immature," "Dad was unfair," "I can understand . . ."). C. S. Lewis says it well:

> Real forgiveness means steadily looking at the sin, the sin that is left over without any excuse, after all allowances have been made and seeing it in all its horror, dirt, meanness and malice, and nevertheless being wholly reconciled to the man who has done it. That and that only is forgiveness.[2]

It should be said that not every hurt needs to be forgiven. Some things need generosity of spirit, a loving willingness to believe the best. Our partner will at times annoy us, disappoint us, slight us. Some things require patience, not forgiveness. We need a healthy sense of perspective and grace.

Second, *own the hurt*. Joseph was a man who knew what it was to weep (42:24; 43:30; 45:2). Those were tears of hurt for the past, and hope for the future. But he did not deny the pain of abuse or the depth of feelings aroused by the encounter with his brothers. If we deny or suppress the reality of the hurt of being sinned against, we are likely to find it hard truly to forgive. Anger itself is not a sin—in fact, we ought to be angry at sin. But if we merely express anger or try to suppress it, it can lead to sin on our part.

Third, *cultivate a divine perspective*. Joseph did not see himself as a victim of circumstances, but as a child of the God who was working out His mysterious purposes in his life. His brothers had sold him to merchants, but "God sent me ahead of you. . . . God sent me. . . . It was not you who sent me but God." Pharaoh had brought him out of prison to become first lord in Egypt but it was not Pharaoh but "God has made me lord of all Egypt." He says it even more eloquently in 50:20: "You intended to harm me, but God intended it for good to accomplish what is now being done."

We will never, this side of heaven, unravel the mystery of God's sovereign purposes working compatibly with human choices and sins. In Joseph's life, we see the outcome. In our own lives we often cannot. But we need to find rest in the sovereignty of God who makes even the wrath of man to praise Him. God's sovereignty doesn't remove the brothers' guilt nor does it resolve the mysteries. But it does make our suffering redemptive—helping us to see that our suffering is not wasted when we allow the Lord to use it.

Fourth, *grant forgiveness*. Joseph does not explicitly say "I forgive you," but almost every sentence conveys that message in a powerful way. He has released them from their debt: "Do not be distressed and do not be angry with yourselves."

Seventeen years later when Joseph's father, Jacob, died, his brothers began to replay the tapes of their old sins:

> *When Joseph's brothers saw that their father was dead, they said, "What if Joseph holds a grudge against us and pays us back for all the wrongs we did to him?" So they send word to Joseph, saying, "Your father left these*

instructions before he died: 'This is what you are to say to Joseph: I ask you to forgive your brothers the sins and the wrongs they committed in treating you so badly.' Now please forgive the sins of the servants of the God of your father." When their message came to him, Joseph wept.

His brothers then came and threw themselves down before him. "We are your slaves," they said.

But Joseph said to them, "Don't be afraid. Am I in the place of God? You intended to harm me, but God intended it for good to accomplish what is now being done, the saving of many lives. So then, don't be afraid. I will provide for you and your children." And he reassured them and spoke kindly to them. (Genesis 50:15–21)

There is something poignant about Joseph's tears in this story. He had truly forgiven his brothers but such a response seemed so remarkable they would not believe it. Joseph had let their sin go; they kept holding on to it. How often we treat God's forgiveness in precisely the same way!

Joseph's brothers made a simple mistake—they thought Joseph had forgiven them for Jacob's sake. In fact, Joseph had done it for the Lord. We need to forgive for exactly the same reason: "forgiving each other, just as in Christ God forgave you" (Ephesians 4:32). The primary reason we forgive is for God—not for ourselves, our marriages, or our partner. Forgiveness is always an evidence of God's grace. It is one thing Satan cannot counterfeit. He has never experienced forgiveness and he has never granted it.

FORGIVENESS IS A DOOR WE OPEN TO THE FUTURE

There is a third dimension of forgiveness—we give it in the present to cleanse the past with the hope of changing the future. Not to forgive is to let the past rule the future, to drag yesterday's chains throughout life.

• Unforgiveness blocks Christ's love in our lives, "but if you do not forgive men their sins, your Father will not forgive your sins" (Matthew 6:15).

• Unforgiveness binds us to the past. Paul warns the Corinthians that if they do not forgive someone who has wronged them, they will be outwitted and taken advantage of by Satan (2 Corinthians 2:5–11). It is a spiritual law: a heart closed to forgiveness is open to satanic oppression.

• Unforgiveness embitters us. The Lord warns that a person who does not forgive is "turned over to the jailers to be tortured" (Matthew 18:34). It is a vivid way of saying that a refusal to forgive is enslaving. Frederick Buechner puts it vividly:

> To lick your wounds, to smack your lips over grievances long past, to roll over your tongue the prospect of bitter confrontations still to come, to savor to the last toothsome morsel both the pain you have given and the pain you are giving back—in many ways it is a feast fit for a king. The chief drawback is that what you are wolfing down is yourself. The skeleton at the feast is YOU.[3]

• Unforgiveness is enchaining, and the chains are woven around the next generation. If ever there was a case of the sins of the parents being visited on the children, it is the passing on of a bitter, unforgiving spirit to one's children. One of Joseph's greatest gifts was to break the family chain.

Joseph not only broke chains, he opened doors:
• He opened a door of liberty. His brothers remained bound by their sin. Joseph was a genuinely free man.

• He opened a door of ministry. Joseph became the healer of his family and the savior of his people. He lives out what Paul describes in 2 Corinthians 1:3–4, "Praise be to the God and Father of our Lord Jesus Christ, the Father of compassion and the God of all comfort, who comforts us in all our troubles, so that we can comfort those in any trouble with the comfort we ourselves have received from God."

• He shut a door of tragedy. Humanly speaking, had Joseph not responded as he did, the nation of Israel would never have come into being. The children of Israel would each have gone their own way, divided by their guilt and destructive behavior.

Joseph lived long ago and far away. But the issue of forgiveness is alive and well, and living in your home. Much of the time it is woven into the fabric of daily life, as two sinful people live with one another. Good marriages require good forgivers, and healthy marriages deal with offenses by developing a healthy habit of owning, confessing, and forgiving sin. But when sins are denied, ignored, or flaunted, a free floating hostility develops.

All too often we are tempted to hold on, to nurse our grievances. Your partner may have hurt you deeply. It is inexcusable sin. Hopefully, repentance is present. But even if it isn't, God calls you to go to him, to forgive, and to begin to reach for restoration. The cost will be high, the pain will be real. But the cost of not forgiving will be far higher.

10

God's Model for Men

IN A SCENARIO REPEATED AROUND THE COUNTRY, more than seventy thousand men converged on the Los Angeles Coliseum for a Promise Keepers conference. The hours that followed left an indelible although invisible mark on nearly everyone present. We prayed, cried, listened, laughed, sang, and cheered together. There were moments of awesome silence; there were times of joyful celebration; there were occasions of spiritual power. We met the Lord and He graciously met us.

As I wandered through the crowds at various times, I was struck by the sheer diversity of the men. Whatever else is true, men who follow Christ have no distinguishing external features of race, class, hairstyle, or age. They don't have a similar body type or clothing style. Christian men are not stamped out of some spiritual cookie cutter. Yet there are some things that ought to be true of every believing man.

The issue of what it means to be a man has become a pressing one in our culture. Appropriate concerns about masculine chauvinism has led to some radical attacks on men per se and to a repudiation of any intrinsic concept of masculinity. Predictably this has led to a reaction on the part of many that see any feminist complaint as foolish or ill-founded.

What does it mean to be a man? In 1990, when PBS broadcast a Bill Moyers program entitled "A Gathering of Men" with Robert Bly, it led to a record response of letters and requests for transcripts and copies. Bly's book, *Iron John,* appeared on the best-seller lists for months. He is a poet and writer, a student of myths and legends, and in his book he chronicles the pain and confusion he sees as part of being a man at the end of this century. Men, he claims, have become more thoughtful and gentle in the last twenty years but at the cost of their vitality and happiness. As he writes:

> In the seventies I began to see all over the country a phenomenon that we might call the "soft male." Sometimes even today when I look out at an audience, perhaps half the young males are what I'd call soft. They're lovely, valuable people—I like them—they're not interested in harming the earth or starting wars. There's a gentle attitude toward life in their whole being and style of living.
>
> But many of these men are not happy. You quickly notice the lack of energy in them. They are life-preserving but not exactly life-giving. Ironically, you often see these men with strong women who positively radiate energy.[1]

Many of Bly's solutions seem bizarre and superficial. But obviously he is touching needs. Tens of thousands of men have headed off into the woods on "Wild Man" weekends to bang drums, dance around a fire, and tell stories. Their quest was to discover the "warrior within," who has been emasculated by society, women, and organized religion.

Robert Bly's insights represent, at best, a fad. But his question is abiding and important. What does it mean to be a man? This is an urgent question in a society where millions of children are brought up with no permanent male presence in their lives. The feminist movement, the macho myth, the playboy ethic, the gay rights movement—these and more have contributed to our confusion. Men are in trouble, and cause trouble. Violent crime, sexual abuse, child abuse, gang warfare, and pornography are all predominantly male based. Something is terribly wrong.

We desperately need a model of what a whole and healthy man looks like. Fortunately, we have such a model in the most fully human and masculine person who ever lived. We do not tend to think of the Lord Jesus like that. I must confess that I have been put off by almost every portrayal of Jesus I have ever seen. Most often He seems wimpy and weak, even fragile. His clothes are always whiter than white, his nails are always clean (a remarkable accomplishment for a third-world itinerant peasant!) and He is only dubiously fully human. He seems feminine rather than masculine.

How could such a figure get twelve men to reorder their lives to follow Him? Have five thousand men (not counting women and children) follow Him into a desert to listen to Him? Intimidate the entrenched establishment of His nation? Face down political strongmen like Pilate and Herod? We need to look at Jesus through fresh eyes or He will vanish into the mists of history and we will lose God's answer to our very modern question: "What does a real man look like?" There are many places we could turn to meet the man Jesus. Let me suggest Luke 9:42–56 as a beginning place:

> *Even while the boy was coming, the demon threw him to the ground in a convulsion. But Jesus rebuked the evil spirit, healed the boy and gave him back to his father. And they were all amazed at the greatness of God.*
>
> *While everyone was marveling at all that Jesus did, he said to his disciples, "Listen carefully to what I am about to tell you: The Son of Man is going to be betrayed into the hands of men." But they did not understand what this meant. It was hidden from them, so that they did not grasp it, and they were afraid to ask him about it.*
>
> *An argument started among the disciples as to which of them would be the greatest. Jesus, knowing their thoughts, took a little child and had him stand beside him. Then he said to them, "Whoever welcomes this little child in my name welcomes me; and whoever welcomes me welcomes the one who sent me. For he who is least among you all—he is the greatest."*

"Master," said John, "we saw a man driving out demons in your name and we tried to stop him, because he is not one of us."

"Do not stop him," Jesus said, "for whoever is not against you is for you."

As the time approached for him to be taken up to heaven, Jesus resolutely set out for Jerusalem. And he sent messengers on ahead, who went into a Samaritan village to get things ready for him; but the people there did not welcome him, because he was heading for Jerusalem. When the disciples James and John saw this, they asked, "Lord, do you want us to call fire down from heaven to destroy them?" But Jesus turned and rebuked them, and they went to another village.

When Carl Sandberg, the poet and Abraham Lincoln scholar, was asked to address Congress on the one hundred and fiftieth anniversary of Lincoln's birth, he said of his hero: "Not often in the history of mankind does a man arrive on earth who is both steel and velvet, who is as hard as rock, and as soft as drifting fog." Another Lincoln admirer, Professor Mark van Doren, observed: "To me, in some ways Lincoln seems the most interesting man who ever lived. He was gentle but this gentleness was combined with a terrific toughness, an iron strength."

Hardness and softness; gentleness and toughness—these are difficult qualities to combine. Lincoln brought them together to a remarkable but flawed degree. But the Lord Jesus joins them in perfection. Thus the Bible portrays Him simultaneously as the Lion and the Lamb. And the man who follows Him will increasingly become like Him.

THE MAN WHO FOLLOWS CHRIST WILL BE A MAN OF STRENGTH

In recent years, it has been politically correct to downplay the differences between the sexes. The political and economic drive to give women equality was often grounded on the premise that "equal means identical." If men and women were to have interchangeable roles, they must be essentially interchangeable beings. But certain stubborn facts of biology will not go away. A *Time* magazine cover story in 1992 asked the question, "Why are men and women different?" The cover answered its own question: "It isn't just upbringing. New studies show they are born that way." Ours may be the only generation in history to consider such information front-cover news!

Recent research has, in fact, helped to delineate some of the differences between men and women. Of course, all generalizations have exceptions and it is all too easy to overstate the differences. After all, men and women have far more in common than they have in distinction. Yet, by divine design, men and women complement one another. These differences are more than cultural, they are creational. Not only do our bodies differ in obvious anatomical ways, our brains are "wired" differently. There are different interconnections between the two sides of the brain between men and women. As a result, we process information and verbalize it differently. Girls develop language skills more quickly than boys and have stronger verbal skills. We even play differently. Researchers have noticed that when children play at recess, boys choose sides based on skill, girls on relationships. When someone is hurt, boys expect the hurt player to get out of the way (if the injury isn't severe) so the game can go on; girls gather around and comfort the hurt girl. Boys argue more about the rules, but their games go on longer, while girls subordinate rules to relationships, and often end the game. Men see success in terms of task and achievement, women in terms of relationship and attachment. Men take pride in tough-minded independence, women in connectedness.

All of this is to say that masculinity is not a culturally induced decoration but a distinguishing fact that imposes itself on every cell of a man's body and on every aspect of his life. But what is the essence of masculinity? Stereotypes abound. The Playboy model tells us that "real men use women." The Patton model tells us that "real men love war" and strut their stuff through violence and power. The Jimmy Johnson model tells us that "real men love to win," whatever the cost.

The Lord Jesus provides a very different model, but it is not the Sunday school Jesus too many of us imagine—a kind of first-century Mr. Rogers dispensing nice words and pious platitudes. The Lord was incredibly strong. He rallied followers, terrified leaders, confronted rulers. But He also loved people, enjoyed parties, inspired loyalty, and poured out deep emotions. He had strength of character—He knew who He was and what His mission was in the face of incredible pressure. He had deep courage. Luke portrays Him facing demons to rescue an oppressed boy. He resolutely sets out for Jerusalem knowing that He faced betrayal, treachery, and brutality. He stood against cultural pressure, which promised great rewards for conformity but a terrible price for resistance. He had the strength of unshakable commitment to the Father's purpose and mission, at the cost of intense suffering. There was iron in His soul.

Yet He never used His strength to bully, coerce, or control. His strength did not separate Him from people. Instead, people approached Him readily and sought opportunities to be near Him. He spoke with a strength of conviction, a clarity of meaning and an integrity of character that set Him apart from other teachers. People heard Him gladly and marveled "at the gracious words that came from his lips" (Luke 4:22). However, He pandered to no one, and entrenched powers shook before His biting words of reproof and correction.

One of the great biblical titles given to the Lord Jesus is "the Lion of Judah." It is a term full of prophetic meaning, proclaiming Him as the promised king from the tribe of Judah, the awaited son of David who would rule as Israel's messiah king. At the same time, it proclaims the innate strength of King Jesus. He is a steel Lion, with an inner strength that emanates from the core of His being.

The strength of the Lion provides a model for men who seek to follow Him. It is a strength to lead, to take the initiative, which comes from being *under* authority. Men who follow Christ do not lead because they love to lead or to get their own way. They lead so that God's will and purposes might be accomplished. The strength of a Christ follower is a capacity to give and to serve. The Lord makes it very clear, by His words and His life, that greatness is all about serving. A godly man provides for others, pursues their best interests, and protects those under his care. He is not afraid of strength but of selfish, self-serving strength.

There is an important insight from the creation account. Adam was specifically given the responsibility to work and care for the garden, before Eve was created (Genesis 2:15). Clearly, the woman shared in this task, but when the judgment falls because of sin, the curse on Adam relates to his work. There is a strong sense, born out of the rest of Scripture and universal human experience, that a man is a problem solver, a provider, who finds great meaning in achievement. Relations do and must matter, but men are created in a special way to provide and protect. This is a special part of the strengths of a man. The problem is that sin misdirects strength, that male strength too often becomes aggression, abuse, and violence, qualities seen too often in our homes and society.

The strength that Christ models is the strength to live a controlled and disciplined life. Movies celebrate the self-indulgent lifestyle of the swaggering men who indulge their sensual appetites freely. "Better a patient man than a warrior, a man who controls his temper than one who takes a city" (Proverbs 16:32). One of the ironies of our time is that we lavish millions of dollars upon men who have learned to discipline their physical bodies in athletic contests. Yet our newspapers record the almost total inability of many of them to discipline their personal lives. True strength also involves the ability to harness one's emotions and energies to worthy ends. As Robert Bly rightly observes:

> The quality of a true warrior is that he is in service to a purpose greater than himself: That is to a transcendent cause. . . . When a warrior is in service to a True King . . . he does well and his body becomes a hardworking servant.[2]

Supremely, the strength of a man is the strength to sacrifice for the good of others. This has been the ideal of manhood through the centuries, the stuff of legends, the source of story and song. Such a mind-set has fallen on hard times recently. The sophisticated mock at such ideas as romantic nonsense or patronizing chauvinism.

Others, addicted to a therapeutic model of self-fulfillment, have set aside notions of sacrifice and self-giving as damaging to the self. Far more, having lost a passion for the glory of God and a zeal for His purposes, have lapsed into a self-exalting apathy. In the early years of the twentieth century, when the unsinkable Titanic met its fate in the icy north Atlantic, the tradition was "women and children first." Almost 80 percent of those who drowned were men, many of whom had given up places in the lifeboats for others. A recent survey indicated that today only 35 percent of men would be willing to give place to women and children, other than their own family. Two-thirds would be willing to give their place to their own wives, but only 54 percent would relinquish their seat for their own mothers! How tragic! It isn't just that the day of gallantry has died. So has a vital aspect of true manhood.

The strength of the Steel Lion was very different. He loved us and gave Himself. Nowhere was He stronger than when He seemed weakest, laying down His life on the cross, bearing our sins, confronting Satan and the demonic forces. A man who is not willing to lead as Christ would lead, to serve as Christ would serve, and to sacrifice as Christ would sacrifice has missed the essence of manhood. Self-protection, self-absorption, and self-service are the antithesis of true strength.

A MAN WHO FOLLOWS CHRIST WILL BE A MAN OF SOFTNESS

There is another dimension to the person of the Lord Jesus. If He is the Lion of the tribe of Judah, He is also the Lamb of God. If He is a man of strength, He is also the man of sorrows, whose heart was open to those around Him. He was caring, able to express love and emotions. He was concerned, willing to show gentleness to those broken by life's hurts or self-inflicted wounds. He was considerate, beautifully fulfilling the Old Testament prediction:

> *A bruised reed he will not break,*
> *and a smoldering wick he will not snuff out.*
> (Isaiah 42:3)

He was committed, moving toward people in their needs and able not only to feel their emotions but to express His own, whether it be grief, anxiety, compassion, or anger. His emotions themselves are rich and richly expressed. He is moved with compassion, filled with indignation, troubled in spirit, overcome with tears, and overwhelmed with sorrow. He is full of joy, tender in love, calm in crisis with inner poise and peace.

The softness of Jesus had nothing to do with weakness. It had a great deal to do with His full involvement in human suffering and weakness. He was born into a family deeply acquainted with suffering—the very circumstances of His birth made that a reality. His childhood was that of a peasant in an occupied country, dealing with the realities of what we today would call a third-world lifestyle. His father died in Jesus' youth, and the gospels suggest that He was in many ways an outsider in His own family, a source of confusion and annoyance to siblings who could not possibly understand who He was (His resurrection transformed their relationship). His adult life was, to say the least, unconventional. Many of us who worship Him enthusiastically would have rejected Him as a candidate for our church's pastoral staff—an untrained, uncredentialed itinerant peasant dependent on others' gifts and surrounded by a ragtag group of followers. But these realities of His life did not make Him hard or bitter. Rather He lived among peasants who struggled for their daily food and entered into their suffering. He welcomed the marginal and the notorious and, while they never felt vindicated in their sinfulness, they did feel loved. He dined with establishment figures and engaged them winsomely, while challenging them directly. He lived a celibate life, but He reached out to women in all walks of life, breaking social conventions and building holy bridges. He saw children as real people and taught their importance.

The list could go on and on. There is a softness about Jesus that parallels His strength. It is not the softness of sentiment. Rather it is the core softness that comes from a heart of love, a mind of wisdom, and a spirit of grace. His was a genuine, not a stained-glass, masculinity. Some portrayals of masculine spirituality strike one as pious frauds or as other-worldly, pie-in-the-sky. Jesus lived with a hard-nosed, down-to-earth spirituality that was grounded in the reality of first-century Palestine. Clearly there was about Him the aura of the eternal, but there was also a this-worldly authenticity that attracted the unlikely and repelled the merely religious.

As the Lamb, He is also the model for a man to follow. He had an honest acceptance of His own needs and vulnerabilities, which He was able to express clearly to His closest friends. He told them when He was tired or hungry or lonely ("my soul is overwhelmed . . . . Stay here and keep watch with me," Matthew 26:38). He breaks the paradigm of the "strong man" who must not disclose his inner feelings to those around him. If the Lord Jesus, the perfect Son of God, felt need to be vulnerable, then I surely share that need. He did not live in isolation but in community; my need is even greater. I am not a self-sufficient person.

Christ-following men also will know a genuine ability to care, protect, and serve those for whom they are responsible. Shortly after the Persian Gulf war, General Norman Schwarzkoff, the commander of the UN forces, appeared on television. At one point, when he discussed the death of troops under his command, tears began to flow down his face. Barbara Walters pounced with the question: "Why, General, aren't you afraid to cry?" "No, Barbara," the general replied with great poise, "I'm afraid of a man who won't cry." Jesus cried. He cried over the spiritual hardness of Jerusalem and at the tomb of His friend Lazarus. He also laughed. We are told that He was "full of joy through the Holy Spirit" (Luke 10:21) and His enemies complained that He was a party goer, "a glutton and a drunkard, a friend of tax collectors and 'sinners' " (Matthew 11:19). Their accusation was false, but it would have been absurd if Jesus had been a "gloomy Gus." He models for us an ability to laugh, to cry, to nurture, to love, to care.

A Christ follower will also be marked by a deep desire for wisdom. Solomon marks a central truth for men: "Wisdom is better than strength" (Ecclesiastes 9:16), and "The glory of young men is their strength; gray hair [a symbol of wisdom] the splendor of the old" (Proverbs 20:29).

Lambs are hardly models of wisdom. But the Lord Jesus is the epitome of wisdom, and this is especially seen in the balance of His character. He was the Lion who, because He was the Lamb, chose not to use His strength against others but for others. He was the Lamb who, because He was the Lion, was strong enough to be gentle. In both ways, He is the model Man.

THE MAN WHO FOLLOWS CHRIST WILL BE A MAN FOR OTHERS

It was Dietrich Bonhoeffer who described Jesus simply but eloquently as "the Man for others." His life was characterized by relationships and those relationships become a model for men twenty centuries later.

Relationships with Women

The Lord never married, but He nevertheless teaches us about a godly relationship to women. He was always respectful to His mother but He was not dominated by her. Even as a young man, at the age of twelve, He staked out His independence (Luke 2:41–51), at the very time we are told that He was obedient to His parents. As a man, He heeds Mary's counsel but does not submit to her directives (John 2). He experiences estrangement from her when she cannot understand His behavior (Mark 3:21, 31–35), but as He hangs on the cross, He carefully provides for her future well-being (John 19:26–27).

In His relationship with other women, Jesus also provides a model. There is much about His being that we cannot fully understand since we do not possess a sinless humanity. He was truly human and fully masculine. That is to say, He was a truly sexual person, although sin had not corrupted His sexual desire. I do not know all that entails, but I do know that He lived with total purity in thought and deed. He treated women with respect and dignity, with a sensitivity that contradicted the norms of a male-dominated, chauvinistic society. He never married, but His behavior toward the church becomes the model for every married man.

Perhaps Dorothy Sayers has said it as well as it can be said as she reflects on Jesus' treatment of women:

> Perhaps it is no wonder that the women were first at the cradle and last at the cross. They had never known a man like this

Man—there never has been such another. A prophet and teacher who never nagged at them, never flattered or coaxed or patronized; who never made arch jokes about them, never treated them as "The women, God help us!" or "The ladies, God bless them!"; who rebuked without querulousness and praised without condescension; who took their questions and arguments seriously; who never mapped out their sphere for them, never urged them to be feminine or jeered at them for being female; who had no axe to grind and no uneasy male dignity to defend; who took them as he found them and was completely unself-conscious. . . . Nobody could possibly guess from the words and deeds of Jesus that there was anything "funny" about women's nature.[3]

Relationships with Children

The Lord was obviously never a human father. But He was an advocate for children. In a society that valued children but kept them in their place (seen but not heard), He both saw and heard them. He held them, welcomed them, talked to them, and set them forth as the epitome of the kingdom: "Unless you change and become like little children, you will never enter the kingdom of heaven" (Matthew 18:3). He was not passive, disinterested, or uninvolved with children.

Few issues are as important in our modern world. To a tragic degree, men have abandoned children. The Industrial Revolution drove a huge wedge between fathers and children, when it pulled men away from home to work in factories and offices. The Family Revolution of the late twentieth century is far worse and it is already yielding bitter fruit. A huge percentage of children live with only one parent (usually their mothers) and a spiraling out-of-wedlock birthrate means that vast numbers of children will never know their biological father. Even if they do, they will lack the model of a stable, strong, loving man who is a transforming presence for good in their lives. The most important predictor for out-of-wedlock births among young girls, for criminal activity among young males, for school drop-out rates and sexual abuse is father absence. It is not the only predictor but it is the most important. Absent men are a huge part of our current social crisis.

Christ-following men care about and care for children. They

invest in their own children with their money, emotional energy, and time. They teach Sunday school, coach sports teams, sacrifice career advancement, and lead clubs so that other children are cared for. They reach out to support single mothers and fatherless children because they believe in the words of James, the half-brother of their Lord: "Religion that God our Father accepts as pure and faultless is this: to look after orphans [the fatherless] and widows [and single mothers] in their distress" (James 1:27). Real men, God's men, care about kids.

Relationships with Friends

This takes us away from our main focus, but it is worth observing that the Lord Jesus initiated and enjoyed friendships. Wherever He was, community developed. He was not a guru at a distance or an instructor behind a podium. He lived with His men, called them His friends, and shared His life with them. There is a very practical relevance of this for marriage. Men need other men in their lives. There are issues and concerns that another man will be able to help me with and give me support in that would otherwise burden my wife. Good male friendships can be powerful supports to a healthy marriage. There have been a multitude of times when, as I have dealt with a couple in crisis, my strongest recommendation was for the husband to be in a strong, honest accountability relationship with another man (or group of men). This is not an option. Men need men.[4]

Relationship with the Father

No relationship was more important to the Lord Jesus than His relationship to His Father. It was the secret and source of all the He did. It reminds us that the greatest need for a man is a relationship with His God. Before Jesus can be our model, He must be our Savior, as we come to Him in heartfelt trust, acknowledging our sin and receiving the forgiveness He has made possible through his death on the cross. As we receive His grace, power, and love, His Spirit begins to work within us to transform us, to take off our old selves with their practices and put on our new selves, which are being renewed in knowledge in the image of their Creator (Colossians 3:9–10).

The Christ follower's picture of the ideal man does not look like the media's portrayals. He does not resemble John Wayne, Harrison Ford, Sean Connery, Tom Hanks, Michael Jordan, or Joe Montana. The man who desires to be God's man, a man of strength and softness, sets in his focus an authentic, realistic picture of his Lord and steps out to become like Him in each area of his life.

11

Help for Husbands

I BECAME A FATHER IN THE OLD DAYS, before technology removed the excitement of wondering whether it would be a boy or girl, or if you were going to be blessed with twins. At that time, husbands were considered a little too unreliable to witness the actual birth process, and so, when events reached their climax, we were shooed away into a waiting room to worry about the health of our wives and to ponder our new responsibilities. When my son was born, I was forced to wait three floors away from the delivery room, and the doctor forgot to send word to inform me—all this at three in the morning!

Whether you are a father or a husband, the most challenging part is to deal with the consequences of what you started. It's often far more tempting to run than to stay and complete what you set out to accomplish. The mark of a man is not what he begins, but what he finishes.

There is a remarkable verse found in 1 Corinthians 7:33. Paul is describing the relative advantages of being married or single. His central point is that singleness is far less complicated because "a married man is concerned about the affairs of this world—how he can please his wife—and his interests are divided." There are many fascinating implications of that verse, but, for our purposes, it is important to note that a married man has two unavoidable responsibilities—to please the Lord and to please his wife. This is not the same as being a "pleaser." A man properly pleases his wife when he carries out his God-given responsibilities toward her. Those are most helpfully spelled out in the famous words of Ephesians 5:21–33:

> *Submit to one another out of reverence for Christ.*
>
> *Wives, submit to your husbands as to the Lord. For the husband is the head of the wife as Christ is the head of the church, his body, of which he is the Savior. Now as the church submits to Christ, so also wives should submit to their husbands in everything.*
>
> *Husbands, love your wives, just as Christ loved the church and gave himself up for her to make her holy, cleansing her by the washing with water through the word, and to present her to himself as a radiant church, without stain or wrinkle or any other blemish, but holy and blameless. In this same way, husbands ought to love their wives as their own bodies. He who loves his wife loves himself. After all, no one every hated his own body, but he feeds and cares for it, just as Christ does the church—for we are members of his body. "For this reason a man will leave his father and mother and be united to his wife, and the two will become one flesh." This is a profound mystery—but I am talking about Christ and the church. However, each one of you also must love his wife as he loves himself, and the wife must respect her husband.*

No man who reads Paul's words carefully can come away feeling unchallenged. It sets out a standard of behavior that requires supernatural aid. And, of course, that is precisely Paul's point. But it is much more than an assignment of duties. Marriage bears a fascinating resemblance to golf: it is harder than it first looks, can be very frustrating, is full of unexpected hazards, can never really be mastered, and is marvelously fulfilling when you get it right. But you are never really free to enjoy golf at a high level until you master the basics. So too with being a husband, and in this passage the Holy Spirit establishes three essentials of being a husband.

GOD CALLS HUSBANDS TO SERVANT LEADERSHIP

It is impossible to read verse 23 without the word *head* jumping off the page: "For the husband is the head of the wife as Christ is the head of the church, his body, of which he is the Savior." It could not be more clearly stated: the husband is the head of his wife. A similar idea is found in 1 Corinthians 11:3. But what does that mean?

The term *head* refers, of course, to a physical part of our bodies. But the head also comes first or at the extremity, and so in the Greek language, the bow of a ship was called its "head," while both the "mouth" of a river or its source (we speak of "headwaters") could be described as the "head" of a river. It all depended on which way one was going. Because what was first often involved leading the way, the term, especially in the Greek translation of the Old Testament, often described a ruler or leader, a person of rank or authority. The comparison between Christ and the husband in Ephesians 5:23 and the reference to a wife's submission in the surrounding verses makes it obvious that "headship" involves leadership and authority.

But what kind of leadership? Here Paul's usage in Ephesians needs to be carefully considered. In chapter 1, he describes the universal authority of the risen Christ in unmistakable terms:

> *That power is like the working of his mighty strength, which he exerted in Christ when he raised him from the dead and seated him at his right hand in the heavenly realms, far above all rule and authority, power and dominion, and every title that can be given, not only in the present age but also in the one to come. And God placed all things under his feet and appointed him to be head over everything for the church, which is his body, the fullness of him who fills everything in every way.* (Ephesians 1:19–23)

Christ is universal Lord, the unrivaled ruler of all things.

Specifically He is Lord "in the heavenly realms," the unseen world of angels and demons. As such, He is "far above all rule and authority, power and dominion," which include demonic powers (see Ephesians 6:12). To say that the risen Christ is "head over everything" is to assert His rule and control. It is an organizational description, which asserts His power.

But, while Christ is head over everything for the church, He is "*head of* the church, his body." Head of describes organic, rather than organizational headship. Christ's relationship to the fallen angels, and even the unfallen angels, is fundamentally different than His relationship to the church. He is intimately linked to the body. The head may lead the body, but it never serves itself at the expense of the body. If you were to see a head, its hair carefully combed, its features carefully attended, wearing the finest sunglasses perched on top of a neglected, untended, unclean, unfed body, you would recognize that something was terribly wrong. Christ is the Savior of the body. He is the undisputed head of the church, but the focus is not on His power over the body, but His provision for it.

Too many discussions of headship carry on as if Paul wrote that the husband is *head over* his wife. They speak of organizational power, military chain-of-command, decision-making authority. I worked as a construction laborer to pay my way through graduate school, and I vividly recall the carpenter who delighted to tell me, "Inrig, on this job you get paid from the shoulders down." That was classic "head-over" authority. But a husband is *head of* his wife. He is to lead, but for the sake of the "body," the one-flesh relationship, and not for himself. That is how a husband fulfills Ephesians 5:21, "Submit to one another out of reverence for Christ." He has a God-given responsibility to lead, a position based not on male superiority or personal worth but on divine appointment. He is to lead by serving and he is to serve by leading. His position is not given so that he can exercise power or impose decisions, but so that he can meet needs.

It is important that Christ is kept in view as the model of headship. Many things could be said but three things seems particularly significant.

First, Christ was not passive but proactive. His leadership is not that of a remote figurehead. The importance of this can be seen in the light of the observations of Pierre Morrell, in a book provocatively entitled *Passive Men; Wild Women*:

Over the last few years I have seen in my office an increasing
number of couples who share a common denominator. The man is
active, articulate, energetic and usually successful in his work.
But he is inactive, inarticulate, lethargic and withdrawn at home.
In his relationship to his wife he is passive. And his passivity
drives her crazy. In the face of his retreat, she goes wild.

Webster's defines these two terms as follows:

Passive: Inactive, yielding, taking no part, submissive, acted
upon without acting in return.

Wild: Not easily restrained, angry, vexed, crazed, in a state
of disorder, disarrangement, confusion.

Of the wives I've seen in therapy none are actually crazed or
disarranged, but a great many are certainly angry, vexed, and
confused. They're also highly intelligent, talented women of all
ages who have become super unhappy in their marriages. No
doubt that's why I see them in my office.

The husbands are also highly intelligent, extremely likable,
and, at least on an economic level, making it. They work hard in
their business and professional lives. They're excellent
providers. (They almost have to be good providers to maintain
our astronomical standard of living.) But, as I said, active as they
may be at work—they seem incredibly passive at home. They are
increasingly impotent, literally and figuratively, with their wives.
And they silently retreat behind newspapers, magazines,
television, and highballs in the home. Or they perhaps not-so-
silently retreat into affairs, weeknight appointments, and
weekend arrangements out the house.[1]

Such husbands—passive, disengaged, inarticulate—cannot claim
the Lord Jesus as their model. He is always moving toward His
church, in love and concern.

Second, Christ was not demanding but serving. Headship is
often used by immature men to justify their selfishness. "I'm the
head of this family, so you'll do what I say." But Christ's headship
has a very different quality. His words in the Upper Room at the
Last Supper need to ring in the ears of all who claim to follow
Him. They capture the Jesus style of headship:

> *Jesus said to them, "The kings of the Gentiles lord it over them; and those who exercise authority over them call themselves Benefactors. But you are not to be like that. Instead, the greatest among you should be like the youngest, and the one who rules like the one who serves. For who is greater, the one who is at the table or the one who serves? Is it not the one who is at the table? But I am among you as one who serves."* (Luke 22:25–27)

Third, Christ was not demeaning but dignifying. Those who followed Him never became smaller or more insecure. John Piper describes the way in which Christlike headship protects dignity and promotes maturity:

> Christ does not lead the church as his daughter but as his wife. He is preparing her to be a "fellow-heir" (Romans 8:17), not a servant girl. Any kind of leadership that in the name of Christlike headship tends to produce in a wife personal immaturity or spiritual weakness or insecurity through excessive control or picky supervision or oppressive domination has missed the point of the analogy in Ephesians 5. Christ does not create that kind of wife.[2]

The comparison to Christ as the head should simultaneously challenge and humble every married man. It calls for every bit of strength and wisdom he possesses. But they will never be enough. A husband acts for Christ; he can never be as Christ. Our headship is limited because we are. The Lord Jesus was never sinful, selfish, ignorant, or shortsighted. I am all of those things and more. Therefore I need to exercise my God-given headship with deep humility before my God and my wife.

GOD CALLS HUSBANDS TO CHRISTLIKE LOVE

The connection between the statement of verse 23, "the husband is the head of the wife," and the command of verse 25, "Husbands, love your wives," is significant. The first statement is an assertion, not an obligation. Husbands are the head of their wives. That is a responsibility given by God. But men are not commanded to lead their wives, as might be expected. Rather, we are commanded to love our wives and the standard of that love is nothing less than the love of the Lord Jesus Christ displayed at Calvary.

For an Ephesian male, hearing these words from the pen of Paul for the first time, this would be unprecedented. It would be rare enough to hear commands addressed to men. In the ancient world, husbands had rights, wives had responsibilities; men had privileges, women had duties. Women too often were used, rather than valued. William Barclay paints the picture in somewhat bleaker terms than a full study of the evidence warrants, but he nevertheless accurately portrays the dark side of life for a first-century woman:

> The Jews had a low view of women. In the Jewish form of morning prayer there was a sentence in which a Jewish man every morning gave thanks that God had not made him "a Gentile, a slave or a woman." The thing which vitiated all Jewish law regarding women was that in Jewish law a woman was not a person, but a thing. She had no legal rights whatsoever; she was absolutely in her husband's possession to do with as he willed. . . .
>
> The position was worse in the Greek world. Prostitution was an essential part of Greek life. Demosthenes had laid it down as the common and accepted rule of life: "We have courtesans for the sake of pleasure; we have concubines for the sake of daily cohabitation; we have wives for the purpose of having children legitimately, and of having a faithful guardian for all our household affairs." The woman of the respectable classes in Greece led a completely secluded life. She took no part in public life; she never appeared on the streets alone; she never even appeared at meals or at social occasions; she had her own apartments and none but her husband might enter into them. It was the aim that, as Xenophon had it, "she might see as little as possible, hear as little as possible and ask as little as possible." The Greek respectable woman was brought up in such a way that companionship and fellowship in marriage was impossible. A man found his pleasure and his friendship outside his marriage. . . . The whole Greek way of life made companionship between man and wife next to impossible. The Greek expected his wife to run his home, to care for his legitimate children, but he found his pleasure and his companionship elsewhere.

> In Rome in Paul's day the matter was still worse. The
> degeneracy of Rome was tragic. . . . But it is not too much to say
> that the whole atmosphere of the ancient world was adulterous.
> Chastity was the casualty of the increasing luxury of civilization.
> The marriage bond was on the way to complete breakdown.[3]

In this context, Paul's words would have an explosive effect.
The command "Husbands, love your wives," goes against
everything his male audience had ever seen or been taught. Paul is
not echoing their culture's view of marriage, he is totally
overturning it and setting in place a new paradigm of marriage
based on the cross.

God calls every husband to *an exclusive commitment to his
wife*. There can be no competing alliances. And such commitment
is to be a heart commitment, a Christlike-love commitment that is
based in the will and not merely the emotions or the affections. The
love of which Ephesians 5 speaks has little to do with fine words. It
has everything to do with hard commitment.

Husbands are also called to *emotional engagement with their
wives*. The love of Christ is not merely volitional; it is also
personal. "May you rejoice in the wife of your youth. . . . May you
ever be captivated by her love" (Proverbs 5:18–19). The call for a
husband is to be personally invested in his wife.

In a study of 737 men and 646 women, Michael McGill came
to some important conclusions about male intimacy:

> Most wives live with and love men who are in some very
> fundamental ways strangers to them—men who withhold
> themselves and, in doing so, withhold their loving. These wives
> may be loved but they do not feel loved because they do not
> know their husbands.[4]

The Holy Spirit's call, "love your wives," is a summons to
build bridges and break down barriers, so that a husband and wife
may experience a growing intimacy and companionship.

The Lord's model of love has already been the focus of our
attention in this book. For our present purposes I want to notice the
three affirmations Paul makes about Christ's love that becomes my
model:

1. *Christ's love led Him to die for the church* (Ephesians 5:25). "Christ loved the church and gave himself up for her." His love was unreserved—He gave all that He was. His love was unselfish —He did not spare himself. His love was unconditional—He did not require us to meet conditions so we could deserve His love.

2. *Christ's love means that He cares for the church* (Ephesians 5:26). He loves "to make her holy, cleansing her . . ." His love was not a single sacrifice but a continual provision, which continues to nurture and serve us.

3. *Christ's love causes Him to become one with the church* (Ephesians 5:27). His goal is "to present her to himself as a radiant church, without stain or wrinkle or any other blemish, but holy and blameless." He not only brings out the best in us, He provides us with His righteousness and becomes one with us. He removes every possible barrier that exists between a holy God and sinful creatures.

GOD CALLS HUSBANDS TO WISE CONSIDERATION

"Husbands *ought* to love their wives," we read. A man owes something to his wife. He has a divine obligation to discharge. The rabbis contended that a man owed his wife food, clothing, and sexual cohabitation. Some added that he owed her a funeral and redemption from slavery. Compared to the Holy Spirit's standard, such ideas seem trivial. A man owes his wife love, love "as their own bodies." A man knows his own body and he acts on what he knows. He knows its hunger and responds by obtaining food. He knows its discomfort and acts to alleviate distress. He feels its pains or pleasures and responds accordingly. The way we love our bodies is by sensing its needs and doing all we can to meet them wisely.

We are called to know our wives like we know our own bodies. A literal reading of 1 Peter 3:7 commands us to live with our wives "according to knowledge." I am to study my wife and become an expert on her needs and desires, her fears and abilities. I need to learn and accept her uniqueness as a woman and as an individual. I need to study and begin to speak her "love language." But knowledge is not enough. I am to treat my wife like I treat my own body. That doesn't mean that I treat her like a man. Rather it commands me to be as tuned to her as I am to myself, and to adjust my behavior to her needs.

Since I feel I am often on the kindergarten level of living with wise consideration toward my wife, it has been useful for me to review the "vowels" (a-e-i-o-u) of consideration:

Affection—words and deeds of care and consideration, the loving expression of my feelings toward her. This is the gift of security, the knowledge that she is loved and valued.

Esteem—the granting of honor (1 Peter 3:7), which shows her that I value her and respect her worth, her feelings, her ideas, and her accomplishments. In so doing I give her the gift of significance. As a wise person once said, "The best way to praise your wife is frequently." Affirmation is a source of pleasure, and it needs to be regular and consistent. Small gifts, spontaneous compliments, and kind deeds nurture a woman's heart.

Involvement—the spending of time, which shows the value I place upon her company. When she becomes an afterthought on my schedule, when I give everything else a higher priority, I ignore one of life's basic principles—the law of the harvest. I cannot sow neglect and reap intimacy. So I need involvement, the gift of companionship.

Openness—the sharing of my inner self. Because we as men learn early to repress our emotions and to control our feelings, we often leave our wives on the outside of much of our lives. I've sometimes done that in my busyness, other times in my pride, or in my reticence or even in my desire to spare her. But openness presents her with one of my most valued gifts, the gift of self.

Understanding—the determination to pay attention to her, to not only listen to but to hear her, to feel with her and to know her. When I truly give her the freedom to reveal herself to me, I bring to her the gift of acceptance.

Years ago, I read the observation that our lives resemble either sand dunes or sculptures. Sand dunes are shaped by influences, while sculptures are shaped by purposes. If my "husbanding" is shaped by my culture or by my circumstances, my marriage will be like a sand dune, with no fixed shape and no stability. But if I respond to God's call, to bring to my wife servant leadership, Christlike love, and wise consideration, my marriage will be a sculpture, resembling more and more the relationship of Christ and the church.

12

The Way of a Woman

T HE VERY FIRST TIME I ever preached at the church I now serve was
an eventful day. It was June 28, 1992, and at precisely 4:58 A.M.
my wife and I were jolted awake by a strange sensation. It was, in
fact, the Landers earthquake, 7.2 on the Richter scale. Three hours
later, a 6.8 temblor followed. It may be hard to believe, but part of my
text that morning was, "After they prayed, the place where they were
meeting was shaken" (Acts 4:31). Just as I was saying "Amen" at the
end of the first service, we got hit with an aftershock! As I said, it was
an unforgettable day! The congregation was so impressed with such
dramatic effects, they decided to invite me to come!

We agreed to move to Redlands despite such a shaky start, and
since then I've learned a lot more about earthquakes. The infamous
San Andreas fault is a near neighbor and every now and then we
are reminded that *terra firma* isn't quite so firm. And even though
the Landers quake didn't cause much major damage, the less
violent Northridge quake of 1994 showed how much destruction
can result when the ground begins to move.

Earthquakes are strange things. Despite all that scientists know,
they can't predict them because tremors aren't the product of one
discrete event, but the result of huge seismic pressures which build
over the centuries. Residents can deny them and wish them away,
but reality is different. You can criticize and attack the geological

147

forces, but they are not deterred. You can build quake-proof shelters and try to absorb the shock, but if the epicenter is beneath the shelter, it won't do much good. So many pack up and leave the area, only to discover another natural disaster awaiting in the form of a tornado, a hurricane, or a flood.

We live on the other side of an earthquake. I don't mean a natural event such as the Landers or Northridge quakes but a cultural phenomenon that has reordered life in the modern world. During the twentieth century, our view of life has been reshaped. Most of the bedrock assumptions and convictions of Western society—our view of morality, truth, history, and theology have crumbled like a Los Angeles freeway in a quake. We can deny the quake, condemn it, hide from it, or try to flee it. The fact remains: it has taken place, and there is no way back to the world that was. As Art Buchwald put it, "Whether these are the worst of times or the best of times, they are the only times we have."

One of the most significant results of the cultural quake was a major change in the understanding of what it means to be a woman and a man. The rules have changed, for better or worse, and the aftershocks are still being felt. But a vacuum persists. The traditional roles have gone, but the replacement roles have proved to be unsatisfying or unrealistic. This is especially true for women. Many of the cutting-edge feminists of a previous time have found themselves retreating from earlier positions because most women were unwilling to follow into an androgeny that denied their essential femininity or into an antimale stance that led to the dead end of a militant lesbianism.

What does it mean to be a woman? That is an unavoidable question in the late-twentieth century and it bears directly upon our understanding of marriage. The vanishing of the traditional role provides an opportunity to look with fresh eyes at what God intended in the first place. Much of the raw materials for that comes from passages we have already considered, in Genesis 1–3. Another passage of great significance is found in Proverbs 31:10–31. While this is a favorite passage for Mother's Day sermons, it has far broader relevance, as it depicts a woman Scripture sets forth as an ideal:

A wife of noble character who can find?
She is worth far more than rubies.
Her husband has full confidence in her
*   and lacks nothing of value.*
She brings him good, not harm,
*   all the days of her life.*
She selects wool and flax
*   and works with eager hands.*
She is like the merchant ships,
*   bringing her food from afar.*
She gets up while it is still dark;
*   she provides food for her family*
*   and portions for her servant girls.*
She considers a field and buys it;
*   out of her earnings she plants a vineyard.*
She sets about her work vigorously;
*   her arms are strong for her tasks.*
She sees that her trading is profitable,
*   and her lamp does not go out at night.*
In her hand she holds the distaff
*   and grasps the spindle with her fingers.*
She opens her arms to the poor
*   and extends her hands to the needy.*
When it snows, she has no fear for her household;
*   for all of them are clothed in scarlet.*
She makes coverings for her bed;
*   she is clothed in fine linen and purple.*
Her husband is respected at the city gate,
*   where he takes his seat among the elders of the land.*
She makes linen garments and sells them,
*   and supplies the merchants with sashes.*
She is clothed with strength and dignity;
*   she can laugh at the days to come.*
She speaks with wisdom,
*   and faithful instruction is on her tongue.*
She watches over the affairs of her household
*   and does not eat the bread of idleness.*

> *Her children arise and call her blessed;*
> > *her husband also, and he praises her:*
> *"Many women do noble things,*
> > *but you surpass them all."*
> *Charm is deceptive, and beauty is fleeting;*
> > *but a woman who fears the LORD is to be praised.*
> *Give her the reward she has earned,*
> > *and let her works bring her praise at the city gate.*

My response, after reading this passage, is always one of tiredness. Just reading about this woman wears me out! But to dismiss her as the first bionic woman, "superwoman," or "super-mom" is to miss the point. She is intentionally idealized. In fact, she becomes the climactic figure of Proverbs, the epitome of wisdom. Wisdom is a quality of God and it is portrayed, lived out, by a woman. That in itself is a high affirmation of woman.

The passage is an alphabetical acrostic poem. That is, each verse begins with a different letter of the Hebrew alphabet. That is an important clue. It tells us that this is poetry, not a reporter's description. Therefore, we are not to focus on the literal details of her behavior so much as on the underlying principles of her life.

It is also obvious that this portrait is class conditioned and culture bound. This is a woman of wealth and social standing who lives in another time and another place. No modern Western woman can reproduce the specifics of her life (or would want to). But it is possible to evaluate and emulate the enduring principles of her life. This is God's portrait of a model woman.

THE WOMAN GOD HONORS IS A PERSON OF STRENGTH

It is extremely important to understand the description of this woman—"a wife of noble character." This is the third time this phrase, literally "a woman of *hayil*," is used in the Old Testament. Boaz says of Ruth, with obvious admiration, "All my fellow townsman know that you are a woman of *hayil*" (Ruth 3:11). In Proverbs 12:4 Solomon asserts, "A woman of *hayil* is her husband's crown, but a disgraceful wife is like decay in his bones.

Translators have not found it easy to turn the phrase, "a woman of *hayil*," into English. The New International Version renders it "a wife of noble character," while others try expressions such as "a virtuous woman," (KJV), or "an excellent wife" (NASB). The essential meaning and usage of *hayil* is "strength." It is used to describe the physical strength of a man (Proverbs 31:3) or a horse (Psalm 33:17), while it can also describe the strength of character that produces valor or courage. David's "mighty men" are "men of *hayil*," brave warriors whose exploits on behalf of David and Israel are worthy of renown (1 Chronicles 11:10). In another context it is the strength or ability that makes a person a leader. Jethro urges his son-in-law Moses to surround himself with "capable men," men of *hayil*, to help him lead the nation (Exodus 18:21, 25). On other occasions, the term describes the strength or power that comes from wealth.

The significance of this should not be missed. The woman God honors is a woman of strength. She is valued not just for her qualities of beauty and grace, although presumably she has those (v. 30), but also for her strength of character and ability. God's ideal is not the frail, demure, dependent appendage of the Victorian ideal. She is rather a helper who corresponds to man, able to help because her gifts are strong and significant.

God honors the woman of strength and it is important to note that her strengths as a woman are not merely a carbon copy of the strengths of a man. Women are distinctively different from men. At first such an observation seems obvious. But for political purposes it became correct to ascribe all gender distinctions, except the obvious biological ones, to socialization. As we have already observed, men and women have far more in common than they do in contrast; nevertheless the differences are real and profound. From a multitude of perspectives scientists underline the distinctiveness of a woman. Anatomically, genetically, endrocrinologically, neurologically—in these ways and more God has stamped "male" and "female" upon us.

Women need to be affirmed in their sense of uniqueness, and they need to be confident in their feminine identity. The most profound distinctiveness lies not in externals of "femininity" but in a God-given inner drive toward relationships. The very creation of woman is a clue. Human relationships exist because the woman came alongside Adam to make them possible: God created woman so that they carry children within them for nine months, bond to them deeply, and then nurture them at their breasts. All of this is profoundly different than what a man experiences. Relationships and nurturing are deeply implanted. In the judgment statement of Genesis 3:16–20, it is significant that the impact on the woman is spelled out in terms of relationships, while the man's is in terms of work. Far too much could be made of this, but it remains true that women view life through a grid of relationships in a way that men do not. Women possess a strong, nurturing, caring relational component that persists through time and across cultures.

Studies indicate that women filter communication through a strong concern for connectedness. Sitting in a stadium filled with seventy-three thousand men at a Promise Keepers conference, I was struck by the distinctiveness of the situation. Men sat and talked, but even more attention was drawn to bouncing beachballs and paper airplanes, group cheers, and the wave. I suspect that a similar stadium full of women would have felt and sounded very different, filled with the buzz of thousands of intense personal conversations. Cross-culturally, women are characterized by verbal expression, empathy, sympathy and nurturance, while men tend to be problem solvers. This is a generalization rather than a universal truth, but it provides a significant insight into "femaleness."

The differences between men and women are not a matter of superiority or inferiority but a divinely intended provision for mutual support and help. The Harvard psychologist Carol Gilligan points out that men and women speak "in a different voice." Men see themselves as mature in terms of independence and mastery. For a man, to be mature is to feel strong within oneself. Women feel maturity in terms of interdependent bonding. Maturity involves warm attachment to others. Women, even highly successful professionals, describe personal success in terms of relationships, rather than simply in terms of professional or academic distinctions. Men, on the other hand, think of success far more in terms of personal achievement. Describing successful, professional women, Gilligan observes:

In response to the request to describe themselves, all of the women describe a relationship, depicting their identity in the connection of future mother, present wife, adopted child or past lover. These highly successful women do not mention their academic and professional distinctions in the context of describing themselves. If anything, they regard their professional activities as jeopardizing their own sense of themselves. . . . Identity is defined in the context of relationships and judged by a standard of responsibility and care.[1]

Some time ago, I was speaking at a conference, and Elizabeth was with me. At the first session, speakers were asked to introduce themselves and their subject for the week, and to build a bridge to the audience. The moment I sat down, Elizabeth nudged me and said, "You didn't mention the children." And I hadn't. I love my children deeply and had taken the speaking engagement to give them a special experience. I just hadn't thought that relationship was relevant to that context. For Elizabeth, that's not true. Her relationships are always relevant, whatever the context. She would have mentioned the children first.

The first time we visited a kibbutz in Israel, we sat through a fascinating description of its history. The kibbutzim were pioneers of Zionism, long before the nation of Israel existed, and they were driven by a socialist ideal, usually brought from Eastern Europe. The communes employed a kind of unisex equality, with interchangeable roles and totally communal care of children. But that was not the present reality on this kibbutz. As the narrator told the story and answered questions, it became clear that women had found the ideal contrary to their deepest desires. They turned down status jobs even when highly qualified, for time at home; overturned communality by bonding closely to their own children; and insisted on more personal time with and care of their own children. On a parallel track, one of the notable social trends of the nineties is the number of women returning to work at home. Between 1985 and 1990, the number of self-employed women working full time from home tripled!

THE WOMAN GOD HONORS IS A PERSON OF PRIORITIES

Femininity in biblical terms is seen in terms of strength, rather than fragility and frailty. But strength must be channeled to be of value. The feminist movement has rightly opened options to women that were previously closed. The problem is that when possibilities multiply, responsibilities often weaken. Therefore it becomes essential to nail down nonnegotiable priorities. The woman of excellence idealized in Proverbs models a life controlled by the important, not just the urgent or the available.

Her core value is spiritual. "A woman who fears the LORD is to be praised" (v. 30). She is the epitome of wisdom precisely because her life revolves around a core of spiritual well-being. To fear God is to think of Him properly, to respect Him deeply, and to obey Him wholeheartedly. The essence of Eve's failure is that she did not fear God enough to obey Him. A woman of strength knows that the triune God must be the source of her strength and that she can live and speak with wisdom (v. 26) only as she orders her life by God's truth.

Her chief concern is character. The qualities of this remarkable woman are catalogued, especially in verses 25 to 27: strength, dignity, foresight, wisdom, faithful instruction (literally, "the law of loyal love"), carefulness, and diligence. The register of her activities is impressive and even exhausting, but her greatest contribution is who she is. Her life is integrated around a godly, sturdy character. We live in a society that values women because of beauty, talents, and personality. Those have their place, but only character endures. "Charm is fleeting"—whether it be the feminine wiles a traditional society teaches or the interpersonal techniques of modern business. "Beauty is deceptive," because it cannot last and it often misleads. But character endures as the basis of a life that leaves a legacy: "a woman who fears the LORD is to be praised."

In her book *Keep Climbing,* Gail MacDonald includes a beautiful tribute from an Algerian about a missionary to North Africa named Lilias Trotter: "She was still and created stillness. She is beautiful to feel near. I love the quiet of her." In a powerful way, a woman of character becomes a "keeper of the moods," a still point in a turning world.[2] No biblical example is stronger than that of Abigail, a woman described as "an intelligent and beautiful woman" (1 Samuel 25:3). At a moment of crisis, it was her character that rescued her husband from a course of foolishness and restrained David from an act of vengeful spite that would have sullied his reputation forever. MacDonald also quotes the observation of Megan Marshall, from her book *The Cost of Loving: Women and the New Fear of Intimacy*:

> For as long as there have been families, women have been experts in the realm of the emotions. Women understood their children's needs before their infants could speak; women soothed men's nerves; women comforted, cajoled, sympathized, loved. Yet a new generation of women have deliberately made themselves strangers to emotion.[3]

Her central commitment is to family. The Proverbs 31 woman is certainly not homebound, keeping house and oblivious to the larger world. Her life reaches out in ever-widening circles of concern and influence. She is concerned with the larger world around her, opening her hands to the poor and engaged in commercial activity. But all that she does radiates from her central commitment to the family. Her interests and skills are integrated around her home, and not merely dispersed into the various channels of life.

A wise woman invests in her husband and children and finds value there. If life is about what endures beyond our lifetime, then family is one of our supreme investments. This is not to disparage other concerns. It is to value and protect the center. Linda Ellerbee, the outspoken television journalist, was a pioneering woman in her industry. She battled personal challenges and citadels of prejudice. But in a television interview with a colleague, Diane Sawyer, she observed, "If I had it to do all over again, I would have told the network no and stayed with my children more often. Corporations don't always keep score, but children do."[4]

Her personal competence is invested. The range of the woman of strength's gifts and abilities would intimidate almost anyone coming alongside her. And those gifts are fully employed in her life. Entrepreneurial gifts involve her in real estate and commercial enterprise. Managerial ability is seen in her administration of her household and business, and in her personal management of her time. Her social and community concerns cause her to open her heart and hands to the poor and needy, while she supports her husband in his role as a civic leader. Her financial skill leads her husband to trust her as she independently carries out her activities, and her intellectual ability is obvious and valued by others. "She speaks with wisdom, and faithful instruction is on her tongue" (v. 26).

But this is not a modern business person, so absorbed in work that other areas are neglected. She is clearly not a model of passivity or dependence. But neither is she the picture of an obsessive person, eagerly determined to carve her place in the world, whatever the cost. Career and material goals are not her supreme goals.

Sometimes we get the impression that we have a duty to our "talents," to maximize them. How we see our abilities is extremely important. They are not toys to be played with. But neither are they idols to be sacrificed to. Hans Selye, the Canadian doctor who pioneered in the study of the effects of stress, describes the focus on individual achievement which subordinates everything else in life to its service. He compares it to a cancer "whose most characteristic feature is that it cares only for itself. Hence, it feeds on the other part of its own host until it kills the host—and thus commits biological suicide, since a cancer cell cannot live except within the body in which it started its reckless, egocentric development."[5]

No, our gifts must be seen as tools to serve a larger purpose—doing the will of God. The woman of wisdom is astute enough to recognize that.

THE WOMAN GOD HONORS IS A PERSON OF RELATIONSHIPS

The third obvious principle of Proverbs 31 is that this is a woman who is investing her life in primary relationships. Her investment in her husband's life is one of the memorable statements of Scripture:

> *Her husband has full confidence in her*
> *and lacks nothing of value.*
> *She brings him good, not harm,*
> *all the days of her life.*

No more positive marital epitaph can be imagined. The statement, "Her husband has full confidence," is literally, "the heart of her husband trusts in her." Heart trust is a marvelous thing, and in Scripture trust is a response we are to direct toward God alone. We are warned throughout the Old Testament not to put our trust in ourselves (Psalm 49:13), in wealth (Psalm 52:7), in military weapons (Psalm 20:7), in political leaders (Psalm 146:3), or in people (Psalm 118:8), but in the Lord Himself. The one exception is here in Proverbs. A husband can trust in a woman of strength, not as a God substitute but as a God-given helper.

The husband's response to such a woman is clear. He is to call her blessed and to praise her: "Many women do noble things, but you surpass them all" (31:29). A man who has a woman of wisdom in his life is under a divine obligation to trust her, release her to use her gifts, and to praise her privately and publicly.

This woman also invests in her children. Far less is said about them than about her husband, which is also a mark of wisdom. The greatest gift children can receive is two parents who love them within a circle of strong spousal love. But the poem describes her as making sure her family is provided with food and clothing and the security of a loving, caring overseer. Her children are aware of the legacy. They "arise and call her blessed" (v. 28). My mother died of cancer in her sixty-sixth year. It was far too early, but one of the things for which I am grateful is that, on the last Christmas she was with us, my brothers and I had the privilege of carrying out verse 28 literally, telling her of how grateful we were for the legacy she had left us.

We have already observed that this woman's relationships reach out in ever-increasing circles. She is committed to the poor, and her community significance is recognized by others: "Let her works bring her praise at the city gates" (v. 31), the place of civic leadership.

The supreme relationship that undergirds all the others is her relationship with the living God. The vitality of her walk with Christ is seen in every dimension of her experience. She is, in fact, a kingdom agent, bringing the presence of the King into every sphere her life touches. That is why the Spirit commands, "Give her the reward she has earned." Within the framework of the entire Scripture, this is a promise that a woman whose life honors God will be honored and rewarded by God. My mother passed away on May 15, 1984. On that very same day, Francis Schaeffer, the great Christian thinker and leader died. My mother lived in virtual obscurity, touching numerous lives but with no public recognition. She had no career and held no leadership positions. Schaeffer's life touched millions and his name is recognized around the world. But when they arrived together in the place of eternal value, I am convinced that my mother received a reward no less grand than Francis Schaeffer. She had faithfully been a woman of strength, carrying out her priorities, investing in relationships in God's will in God's place to God's glory. So she left behind people who called her blessed and went to meet her Lord who called her faithful.

It is not an easy thing to be a woman in the modern world. Nor was it in the ancient world, when being a Christ follower for many women meant living against the grain of culture and tradition. One early opponent of the gospel, a skeptic named Libanus, looked on with consternation and declared, "What women these Christians have!" Women who gain their sense of femininity not from prevailing culture or lingering tradition but from a vital relationship with the living and true God will always have that effect.

13

A Word to the Wives

Aparty of civic dignitaries was touring a major urban construction project. As the mayor and his wife made their way through the building site, she saw a face that looked strangely familiar. When she went over and introduced herself, she discovered to her amazement that it was her long-lost boyfriend, the man she'd almost married when they were impetuous teenagers. They caught up on the past. The years had obviously been hard on him and now he was trying to get back on his feet, beginning over again as a construction laborer. About that time her husband came over and she introduced them.

As they walked away, her husband had a sly smile on his face. Finally he chuckled and blurted out, "Imagine that. So that's John. If you married him, you'd be the wife of a construction worker." And with a twinkle in her eye she responded, "No, my dear. If I had married him, I'd be the wife of a mayor."

Not every wife is quite so sure that she's the reason for her husband's success. But only a fool would minimize the impact for good a wife can have upon her husband. Scripture doesn't. God created the first woman to be the helper corresponding to man so that together they could carry out the mandate of God. "He who finds a wife finds what is good and receives favor from the LORD" (Proverbs 18:22). "Houses and wealth are inherited from parents but an prudent wife is from the LORD" (Proverbs 19:14). "An excellent wife is the crown of her husband" (Proverbs 12:4 NASB). "The wise woman builds her house" (Proverbs 14:1). But there is another side as well: "With her own hands the foolish one tears hers down" (Proverbs 14:1). No woman sets out to tear down either her husband or her home. But without wisdom that may be the result. Good intentions and intense emotions are not enough.

What does it take to be a wise wife? That is Paul's concern in Ephesians 5:22–33. These are familiar verses but they often are taken out of context and studied as if they stand alone, as the biblical perspective on marriage. In fact, they are part of an extended discussion that begins with the appeal, "Be very careful, then, how you live—not as unwise, but as wise . . ." (Ephesians 5:15). The specific instruction to wives (vv. 22–24) and husbands (vv. 25–33) are an elaboration of what wisdom looks like in a husband or wife.

> *Submit to one another out of reverence for Christ.*
> *Wives, submit to your husbands as to the Lord. For the husband is the head of the wife as Christ is the head of the church, his body, of which he is the Savior. Now as the church submits to Christ, so also wives should submit to their husbands in everything.* (Ephesians 5:21–24)

As a modern person reads Paul's words, the term *submit* jumps off the page like a flashing red light. It conjures up, on one hand, pictures of women's subjugation and second-class status, inferiority and oppression. On the other hand, it connotes powerlessness and victimization. Terrible things have been done in the name of submission; some see it as a synonym for abuse.

While the concerns are real, *submission* is a biblical word, and we must honestly consider its meaning for us today and be faithful to God's revelation. But I have a deep conviction that, if we begin with the term *submit*, we will misunderstand Paul and distort marriage. The one-flesh relationship of a husband and wife isn't primarily about rules and roles. If we see it in those terms we will produce deeply conflicted marriages, where a battle for power rages; dysfunctional marriages, where one partner is controlled or manipulated; or polite and formal marriages, where both partners treat each other like pampered house guests, but where passion and warmth are noticeably absent. None of those are God's intention. That is why, before we look at the matter of submission, we need to consider the implications of verse 21 for both partners, and the larger concept of a wife's role suggested by Ephesians 5.

ESSENTIAL INGREDIENTS: THE MAKINGS OF A HEALTHY MARRIAGE

Suppose I were to hand you a sack of potatoes, a jar of peanut butter, and a gallon of ice cream, and ask you to bake me an apple pie. You would obviously consider me somewhat deranged. You can't bake an apple pie unless you have the right ingredients and then combine them properly, under the right conditions. It should be no less obvious that you cannot have a healthy marriage unless you have the proper ingredients. A man, a woman, and a marriage license are not enough. Implicit in the statement "submit to one another out of reverence for Christ" are three essential ingredients.

First, the partners in a healthy marriage are Christ centered. Reverence for Christ controls the home. Reverence is a product of repentance. When I see God for who He is, and myself for who I am, it leads to a heartfelt acknowledgment of sin and failure. Humility before God causes me to trust His promise of forgiveness and plants in me a desire to please and obey Him. Reverence for Christ puts in me a repentant, humble heart, what David called "a broken and contrite heart" (Psalm 51:17), and what Isaiah speaks of as being "humble and contrite in spirit" (Isaiah 66:2). Proud people are hard to live with. When I lose sight of the cross, I get a beam in my own eye but still want to pick the speck out of Elizabeth's eye. But when our hearts are tuned to Christ, they are also tuned to one another.

A reverent home is also one in which the example of Christ shapes my behavior. I do what pleases Him because reverence involves imitation. As well, the Spirit of Christ empowers those who revere Christ. "Keep on being filled with the Spirit," the command of Ephesians 5:18, occurs when I submissively open my life to Christ. Where Christ is truly revered, the freshness and freedom of the Spirit is fully known.

Second, the partners in a healthy marriage are "oneness focused." The basic assumption of Ephesians is that God, by His Spirit, has brought about something new in Christ. All believers are one in Christ, and that obviously is doubly true of two Christ followers who are joined in marriage, sharing a one-flesh relationship. The abiding principle is to "make every effort to keep the unity of the Spirit through the bond of peace" (Ephesians 4:3). Peter speaks of marriage partners as joint "heirs of the gracious gift of life" (1 Peter 3:7). As we saw in Genesis 2, God's plan is not two people who are enmeshed and melded so that their uniqueness is lost. It is rather two who are joined interdependently so that synergy results. "Oneness" thinking is not uniformity thinking, but harmony thinking. Our concern about distinct roles for husband and wife must never obscure the essential oneness God has established.

Third, the partners in a healthy marriage are servant minded. We are to "submit to one another out of reverence for Christ." In view of what Paul goes on to say about husbands and wives, it is obvious that Paul does not understand that husbands and wives have interchangeable roles. Mutual submission is, in fact, mutual servanthood, a deep commitment to one another that puts the other's needs first. Mike Mason has captured well the unique mindset the Spirit establishes: "Marriage at its best is a sort of contest in what might be called 'one-downsmanship,' a backwards tug-of-war between two wills equally determined not to win."[1]

A WISE WIFE UNDERSTANDS HER ROLE

There is a great deal of discussion about a woman's role in marriage, and much of the discussion centers on Ephesians 5 and parallel statements in passages such as Colossians 3:18, Titus 2:4–5, and 1 Peter 3:1–6. Both traditionalists and feminists, hierarchicalists and egalitarians, turn with great energy to these passages. But there often exists a fundamental confusion about the concept of "role."

When I write a job description for a staff position in the church I pastor, one part of that description describes the job itself—the tasks and duties involved—while another part describes the authority structure—the person or people to whom the staff member is accountable. The two are not identical. A secretary's role is not to submit to the office manager, but to do secretarial duties. Her responsibility is to do her job; her accountability, however, is specifically to her supervisor. In the operating room a lead nurse is accountable to the surgeon. But she has a role, a job assignment to carry out on her own. In the same way, a school principal has a role, a task to carry out. She also has an accountability relationship to her superintendent and school board.

A great deal of confusion comes when we describe a wife's role as that of submitting to her husband. The idea is often given that a wife is simply to do what she is told, while her husband gives orders. All too often the headship of the husband becomes the head trip of chauvinism. This is not to deny the biblical concept of submission. It is to say that submission is an accountability description more than a role description.

A second piece of role confusion is to imagine that a wife's role involves a specific division of domestic tasks. Within Scripture itself, the division of labor differed in different places and circumstances. An agricultural society is a different place than an urban, industrial society. Much of what we now call traditional roles is culturally and historically conditioned, rather than biblically commanded. And often there is great inequity. Studies indicate that working women carry responsibility for 80 percent of household chores. This is not to suggest that Scripture has no directives. It is to insist that Scripture, and not merely custom, must be our guide. Some traditional roles only emerged at a specific point in human history. They are not the way things always have been, nor are they the way God intended them to be.

What is a wife's role? Genesis 2 indicates that she is to be "a helper suited for her husband," bringing her skills and abilities alongside him. Proverbs 31 sees in her a woman of strength and skill, with unique personal qualities. Adam describes his wife in Genesis 3:20 as "the mother of all the living." This is obviously true historically. But it also suggests the unique role of a woman as a nurturer, a person uniquely entrusted by God with a specialty for relationships.

Before the apostle calls a woman to relate to her husband as a wife in Ephesians 5:22, he has addressed her as a believer. She is to live a life of love (5:1–2), to live as a child of light, with moral purity, financial integrity, and godly character (5:3–15), and to live as a person of wisdom, doing the will of God and filled with the Spirit (5:16–21). A woman is to live as a kingdom agent, enlarging the honor of King Jesus, and bringing His presence to bear on her world. A woman's job description is not given to her by her husband but by her Lord.

A WISE WIFE RECOGNIZES HER ACCOUNTABILITY

There is a display in the San Diego Zoo that always intrigues me. It is a two-headed snake. Posted on the window is the description of the snake with this observation: "Animals with two heads lack the intelligence to cooperate with themselves and will die at an early age." The only reason the captive snake survives is that one of the heads submits to the other. Two-headed marriages probably don't do much better. Someone has observed that even a two-car parade will lapse into confusion if someone doesn't take the lead.

The term consistently used in the New Testament of a wife's accountability is *submit*. It is possible to write off Peter's and Paul's words as a misunderstanding or misrepresentation of the Lord, but such an approach robs Scripture of its God-given authority. This is ultimately the Holy Spirit's term. The original Greek word is *hypotasso,* which means "to rank under," "to come under authority." It is not the word for "obey" (*hypakouw*), which is used of children's responsibility to parents. *Hypotasso* is often used in military contexts to describe soldiers who are "under rank," or troops that are in a support position.

However, it is a fundamental principle of interpretation that the way a word is used reveals its meaning. Words have meaning in context. Therefore, we need to study usage and context every bit as much as a dictionary. In the New Testament, *submit* is used in a wide variety of contexts:

- the Son (the Lord Jesus) is submissive to the Father (1 Corinthians 15:28)
- Jesus is submissive to his parents (Luke 2:51)
- citizens are submissive to government (Romans 13;1, 5)
- congregational members submit to church leaders (1 Corinthians 16:15–16)
- spiritual powers submit to the Lord Jesus (1 Peters 3:22)
- demons submit to disciples (Luke 10:17)
- the church submits to Christ (Ephesians 5:24)

Two important observations emerge from these uses. First, it is clear that the nature of a relationship determines the expression of submission. The submission of demons to disciples is very different than the submission of the coequal Son to His loving Father. The submission of the church to its leaders is not the same as the submission of Roman subjects to the dictator Nero. This is of special significance. Marriage is not a military or a business relationship, but a one-flesh relationship based on mutual love and self-giving. Marital submission is not like military submission.

Second, some submission is coerced; marital submission is chosen, and given voluntarily. "Wives, submit to your husbands" is not "Husbands, cause your wives to submit." A beautiful parallel is found in 1 Chronicles 29:24. When David appoints Solomon king in his place we are told that "all the officers and mighty men . . . pledged their submission [gave their allegiance] to King Solomon." The Greek translators chose the verb *hypotasso* to describe a commitment of loyal support. They voluntarily devoted their strength to David's son. It was a passionate, purposeful, joyful pledge of allegiance.

Several scholars contribute to our understanding of submission:

"[It] involves a readiness to renounce one's own will for the sake of others" (Gerhard Delling).[2]

"[This is] an appeal to free and responsible agents that can only be heeded voluntarily but never by the elimination or breaking of the human will, not to speak of servile submissiveness. . . . It is a voluntary attitude of giving in, cooperating, assuming responsibility and carrying a burden" (Markus Barth).[3]

"[It is] a voluntary submission of oneself to others, putting the interests of others above one's own, preferring to give rather than to receive, to serve rather than to be served. . . . It means a giving of oneself to and for others. It is in fact to follow in the steps of him who for the sake of his brethren went to the cross. . . . It does not mean yielding an unquestioning obedience to others, that is something quite different" (C. B. Cranfield).[4]

It is in this light that a wife's sense of accountability operates. She voluntarily devotes her strength to her husband in the context of a one-flesh relationship. She possesses the opposite of a rebellious, self-assertive spirit. Instead there is a holy disposition to yield and support. There is a marvelous description of Maria Taylor, the woman who was Hudson Taylor's godly partner in the establishment of the China Inland Mission (now called Overseas Missionary Fellowship). She became the backbone of the mission because of the value her husband placed on her judgment and her prayer life. J. C. Pollock describes their relationship:

> Hudson could lean hard on her, drawing vigor from her spiritual maturity, her tranquillity and faith, her unwavering affection. Ten years after engagement they were still passionately in love with each other. She gave him and their work all she had, every ounce of strength, every thought that crossed her intelligent mind, all the force of her love. She allowed him to drain her, and if sometimes his demands were unconsciously selfish, she was no more aware of it than he.[5]

Submission is all about sincere and godly support.

1. *Submission involves delegated authority, not personal worth.* Submission is not an expression of a woman's inferiority. What is involved is positional authority, which God has entrusted, for His own reasons, to husbands. The Lord Jesus is coequal with the Father, yet He submits in love, and in His earthly life He submitted to His parents and even to evil government officials (He paid taxes and allowed Pilate and Herod to judge Him). Wives are to submit because it is the will of God, not because they are weaker or more foolish.

2. *Submission involves wise support, not mindless obedience.* The instructions of Peter to wives with pagan husbands presuppose that they did not follow their husbands' religion or morality, a striking break with conventional wisdom. Sapphira is held accountable for her complicity with her husband Ananias in lying to the Holy Spirit (Acts 5:1–22). She was wrong in following her husband. Wives are accountable first to God, then to their husbands.

3. *Submission involves loving service, not servile compliance.* A wife stands under a prior command in Ephesians—to live in wisdom, and to understand what the Lord's will is (5:15–17). She is not called to be a doormat to abusive behavior. Nor is she called to be compliant and silent.

4. *Submission involves activity and not passivity.* A wife is to be a helper, and the model of the Proverbs 31 woman indicates how much energy and initiative that can involve.

5. *Submission is ministry, not manipulation.* Leonard Bernstein was once asked which was the most difficult instrument to play. "Second fiddle," he responded. "I can get plenty of first violinists, but to find one who plays second violin with as much enthusiasm, now that's a problem. And yet if no one plays second, we have no harmony." The purpose of submission is a harmonious blending of gifts and talents.

Paul concludes his challenge to wives with the challenge, "and the wife must respect her husband." Submission is ultimately an attitude of respect, first for the Lord, then for one's husband. A wife who respects her husband affirms his strengths. She becomes an oasis where he can flourish. Respect also means that she helps him manage his weaknesses. She would rather support him than expose him. A woman who truly respects her husband will respect herself, striving to develop her gifts and abilities so that she may become the helper God intended her to be and that her husband needs her to be.

I am a grateful man. The Lord has given me a wife who truly has been a wonderful source of love, support, and encouragement. A few years ago I tried to express to her in poetry the ways in which she modeled Christ to me.

ELIZABETH MY RIB

God fit you for me
     -building your fullness to fit my hollowness
     -moulding your strengths to meet my weaknesses
     -tempering your gentleness to answer my hardness
     -creating your sensitivity to overcome my blindness
     -growing your spirituality to challenge my carnality
Seeing my need, He brought you to me
This gift of love to fill my heart and make me whole
One flesh with you to satisfy created desire
But deeper, far, to become in Him one, spirit and soul
I know what Adam felt
     -running to embrace the woman God had made for him
     -praising His wisdom and His gracious heart of love
     -having found in Creation no other that could be his
      helper but finding in her God's special one
I know what God meant
     -when He called Adam's aloneness something not good
     -but He called His couple something very good
     -delighting His heart in the new thing He had made
I know what Lemuel enjoyed
     -in you my heart trusts
     -of you my tongue boasts
     -for you my being yearns
     -through you my joy flows
     -because of you my soul sings
     -with you my future shines
I love you, and today again I give myself
to you, to be God's man for you.

14

Sex and the Glory of God

THERE IS A PART OF ME that loves the absurd. Probably that is why I love reading about some curious laws that remain on the books in various parts of North America. Some are obviously relics of the past, and time has made them look foolish. Others make you wonder what inspired them in the first place. For example, did people in Lexington, Kentucky, really need someone to tell them not to carry an ice cream cone in one's pocket? Or in Lawrence, Kansas, was it necessary to make it illegal to walk down the street with bees in your hair? I can see the logic behind the law in Danville, Pennsylvania, requiring that all fire hydrants be checked out one hour before every use. I'm just not sure how you work out the timing. Canada, in its wisdom, has made it illegal to board or to leave a plane in flight except to make a parachute jump, in which case you need to be wearing a parachute.

Some of my favorite laws are designed to protect our non-human friends. Therefore, it is against the law to hunt camels in Arizona, to tie a giraffe to a signpost in Atlanta, or to chain a crocodile to a fire hydrant in Michigan. You must not throw a reptile at someone in Toledo, kick the head of a snake in Oregon,

169

blindfold a cow near a public highway in Arkansas, or tease a skunk in Minneapolis. One must not molest a Monarch butterfly in Pacific Grove, California, or let a chicken cross a road in Dartmouth, Nova Scotia. Neither can you tie a pig to a tree in a public place in Kingston, Ontario, or wash a pig in a lane in Big River, Saskatchewan. One must not send a telegram threatening a bird in Canada, and watch your behavior in Connecticut, where it is illegal to entice someone else's bees.

There are many different kinds of laws in the world. Some are serious and some are silly. Some are good, while some are outdated. Some are built into the fabric of nature (the law of gravity), while others are relics of the past and have no lasting relevance.

What kinds of laws are sexual and moral laws? Are they social and cultural conventions, the legacy of the past that may no longer match present reality? Are they religious taboos, the product of superstition or religious control? Are they changeable guidelines, the evolving standards of human nature? Or are they laws of nature, part of the fabric of the way things are, so that to violate them is to invite disaster?

Our culture has largely decided that sexual and moral laws are, at best, relative. They may reflect personal values, cultural tradition, or accumulated wisdom, but they are not absolutes. And Christians agree that many sexual moral standards are cultural and relative. But they also believe that God has established absolute standards that are neither negotiable nor changeable. They are fixed in the way God has made us and are intended for our good. In the unrelenting pressure of a secular society, we need to think carefully and clearly about our moral standards. It is popular in our time to speak of traditional values. But there is little safety in that phrase. "Values" are ultimately evaluations, estimations of worth, and tradition is full of tragic failures. The only firm anchor in the moral floodwaters of our time will be biblical virtues, standards of behavior that conform to God's character and requirements.

Someone has claimed that the average high school student today faces more sexual temptation on his way to school in the morning than his grandfather could find if he went looking for it on a Saturday night. There is a remarkable parallel between our times and biblical times, especially the period when the church was established in places like Corinth. The Corinthians of the first century were the Californians of the twentieth—people living in a sensual, permissive, indulgent society. They could no more hide from sexual temptation than we can.

Therefore Paul's words to them have special relevance to us as he describes the pathway of sexual purity in a morally polluted society:

> *Do you not know that the wicked will not inherit the kingdom of God? Do not be deceived: Neither the sexually immoral nor idolaters nor adulterers nor male prostitutes nor homosexual offenders nor thieves nor the greedy nor drunkards nor slanderers nor swindlers will inherit the kingdom of God. And that is what some of you were. But you were washed, you were sanctified, you were justified in the name of the Lord Jesus Christ and by the Spirit of our God.*
>
> *"Everything is permissible for me"—but not everything is beneficial. "Everything is permissible for me"—but I will not be mastered by anything. "Food for the stomach and the stomach for food"—but God will destroy them both. The body is not meant for sexual immorality, but for the Lord, and the Lord for the body. By his power God raised the Lord from the dead, and he will raise us also. Do you not know that your bodies are members of Christ himself? Shall I then take the members of Christ and unite them with a prostitute? Never! Do you not know that he who unites himself with a prostitute is one with her in body? For it is said, "The two will become one flesh." But he who unites himself with the Lord is one with him in spirit.*
>
> *Flee from sexual immorality. All other sins a man commits are outside his body, but he who sins sexually sins against his own body. Do you not know that your body is a temple of the Holy Spirit, who is in you, whom you have received from God? You are not your own; you were bought at a price. Therefore honor God with your body.*
> (1 Corinthians 6:9–20)

Paul is not writing to people for whom sexual issues were merely academic problems. Homosexuals, adulterers, sexually promiscuous—"that is what some of you were." And although they had experienced the redeeming grace of God which had cleansed their past and given them a new heart and a new start, this did not mean that their ingrained sinful appetites were immediately removed or that their surrounding environment was miraculously transformed. They continued to struggle with their colorful sexual history and their pervasively and permissively sexual environment. Salvation makes us new people in Christ; it does not erase all past habits.

WE LIVE IN A CULTURE THAT IS SEXUALLY OBSESSED AND CONFUSED

A member of President Clinton's cabinet was eventually forced to resign for her consistent pattern of outrageous comments. Her response to her critics was that their opposition showed that we live in "a repressed Victorian society that needs to learn that sex is good and pleasurable." Her comment was astonishing. Whatever else may be true, our problem isn't sexual repression. Sexual obsession, perhaps. Sexual behaviors that other generations would only have whispered about are openly flaunted and imported into our homes by television. Sexual purity is mocked as outmoded and unnatural. And any idea that moral misbehavior has significant personal consequences is scoffed. Of course sex is good and pleasurable, but good and pleasurable things (such as water, fire, and electricity) can be misused and become the causes of great damage. That is what has happened in our times.

Paul's concern in these verses is not sex but sexual immorality (the Greek term is *porneia*). *Porneia* describes all sexual intercourse outside of marriage, whether it be premarital sex (fornication), extramarital sex (adultery), homosexuality, or perversions such as incest or pedophilia. It is the most general term to describe sexual sin and he simply commands, under the direction of the Holy Spirit, "Flee from *porneia*, sexual immorality." As one scholar observes, "The New Testament is characterized by an unconditional repudiation of all extramarital and unnatural intercourse." Thus 6:12–20 is concerned primarily about how we *must not* use sex. In chapter 7:1–7, his focus is on how we *must* use our sexual being in marriage: "Do not deprive each other" (v. 5). The overarching principle is found in 6:20: "Therefore honor [or glorify] God with your body." Our sexual capacity brings glory to God when we use it in a way consistent with His purposes.

Paul is writing to a people whose culture minimized *porneia*. Sexual sin was viewed as an oxymoron. Corinth had a reputation as the most indulgent city in the ancient world. Even today, when visiting a museum in Corinth or Athens, you become aware of how pervasive sensuality was in Paul's day. Corinth was a seaport with all the temptations common to such cities. But it was also famed for its beautiful temple of the love goddess, Aphrodite, with her squadron of more than a thousand temple prostitutes. Its statuary is full of exaggerated sexual organs. There was virtually nothing in the society to discourage indulgence. The specific cultural beliefs encouraged physical pleasures of all kinds, saw them as having no moral significance, and mocked concepts of celibacy. "Chastity," said Seneca, "is simply a proof of ugliness."

The parallels between their times and ours are self-evident. Our culture is increasingly Corinthian. We live in a time of sexual slogans which carefully avoid moral judgments: people are sexually active (never promiscuous); movies are sexually explicit and "adult" (never perverse or degrading); individuals have "sexual preferences" (rather than sexual sins). We are a law unto ourselves—freedom and rights make the individual autonomous. Combined with our culture's sexual obsession, our moral vacuum makes indulgence attractive. But it is a descending spiral. Our pursuit of sexual pleasure both as individuals and as a society causes past pleasures to be less fulfilling or arousing, and so we fall into a pursuit of new experiences which plummet into deeper degradation and addiction.

If sexual obsession makes indulgence attractive, our sexual confusion makes temptation pervasive. No one needs to go far to find it. I have heard too many stories of vulnerable people who have found willing partners; seductive people who have ensnared others; naive people who entered a course of behavior that was soon out of control; respectable people who have a secret life full of pornographic addictions. The Corinthian motto was "everything is permissible for me"—a thoroughly modern sentiment.

We live in a culture full of bumper-sticker morality: "If it feels good (and he or she consents), do it"; "whatever turns you on"; "Don't impose your values on me." There are three basic ideas that underlie such slogans. First, there are no sexual absolutes. Second, sexual standards are values, not divine laws. Third, sexual behavior is private and personal. We are sovereign over our own bodies.

Paul faces this Corinthian attitude head-on. First of all, he insists that the concept of freedom behind it is confused. There is a naive truth in the slogan, "Everything is permissible for me." There is a proper use for every created thing. But while the use of my body is personal, it is never truly private. It never affects me alone. That is why, for Christians, freedom is *never* the supreme good. My life affects others. Therefore, edification, building up rather than using others, must be my goal. Nothing is more intensely selfish than lust. The language of seduction and the language of indulgence may use the words of love but they destroy the grammar of love. Lust makes me the subject and the other person the object; love reverses the pattern.

Sexual indulgence promises freedom. It proves to be enslaving and addicting. "Everything is permissible for me—but I will not be mastered by anything." The promise of sexual freedom is appealing; the results are appalling. Despite all the talk of sexual liberation in the past thirty years, there is pathetically little sense of fulfillment. Our stars and celebrities leave behind them a tragic legacy of broken marriages, addictive behaviors, and emotional traumas. We have spawned a society in which sexual abuse is rampant, pornography is epidemic, sexual violence is increasing, broken marriages are pervasive, and deviant behaviors are accelerating. Add to this the spread of sexually transmitted diseases, the reality of AIDS, and the time bomb of increasing illegitimacy rates (the children aren't illegitimate; their parents are!). If this is freedom, I would hate to experience bondage! And what is true socially is all the more true personally. Adultery is sin, no matter how attractive it appears, and it will grow bitter fruit. So too will all kinds of *porneia*, including that of the mind.

The Corinthian confusion about freedom was that freedom means indulging desires. Their confusion about the nature of sex is equally modern. Sex is a purely natural function, they claimed, like eating. "Food is for the stomach and the stomach for food," was their motto, implying that sex is like food. Food is not a moral issue, they contended. It is a natural provision with no moral consequences. So, too, with sex. Hugh Hefner, the *Playboy* magazine founder, says it directly: "Sex is a biological necessity. Find yourself a likeminded partner and let yourself go. It is no different than eating or drinking."

Paul tells us that such thinking is incredibly naive. Sex is personal, not just physical. A bad meal may affect my digestion; but sexual behavior will involve my essential person. Hefner, of course, knows that. He doesn't put sirloin steaks in his centerfolds, but naked women. Good food is wonderful, but no one has a relationship with ravioli. But food prepared or stored wrongly can kill the body. Sex used outside of God's plan will surely wound the soul, and it may murder a marriage.

WE ARE CALLED TO SEXUAL PURITY

But God's standard of sexual behavior goes far beyond merely avoiding sin. His restrictions are always invitations to a God-honoring, life-enhancing pattern of life. When Moses calls Israel to a lifestyle of obedience to God's revealed requirements, his appeal is "now choose life," because God's desire is for us to experience "life and prosperity" rather than "death and destruction" (Deuteronomy 30:15, 19). God's standards are not denials, but invitations to a way of life that pleases God and produces a life not only free from regret but full of true pleasure.

We are called to sexual purity *because of the nature of our bodies*. Simply put, our bodies matter to God. The ancient Corinthians were taught by their philosophers that their bodies were the prison house of the soul. Christians view the body very differently, and Paul tells us three crucial facts about them. First, our bodies *matter* to the Lord: "The body is not meant for sexual immorality, but for the Lord, and the Lord for the body." Our bodies are for the Lord. They exist to bring Him pleasure and further His purposes in the world. Our culture tells us human beings are for sex; our sexual drives are lord. Scripture teaches sex is for human beings; Christ is Lord. And the Lord is for the body. He is not antiphysical. He created our bodies, sanctified and blessed their desires and functions, and purposes to raise them when Christ returns. If our bodies matter to God, then what we do with them matters. Second, our bodies *belong to* the Lord: "Do you not know that your bodies are members of Christ himself?" Our physical bodies, as an intrinsic part of our true selves, were purchased at Calvary, and in a mystical way our physical being gives visible expression to the Lord's presence in the world. Hence Paul's questions: "Shall I then take [a term of physical force: "snatch in rebellion"] the members of Christ [our sexual organs] and unite them with a prostitute?" Obviously not. The issue is not specifically prostitution (the most common form of immorality in Corinth) but sexual sin. The third fact is that my body contains the Holy Spirit. He lives within every child of God. Therefore, my sinful use of my body implicates the Trinity: "Do you not know that your body is a temple of the Holy Spirit, who is in you, whom you have received from God? You are not your own." Every individual believer is a special dwelling place of the eternal God.

It is hard to imagine any more emphatic way to express the importance of our bodies and the validity of our physical appetites. God is for the body. He has included it within the work of salvation. Our body is not only destined for resurrection, it is here and now the dwelling place of God. My sexual conduct matters to God and can honor and glorify Him.

We are also called to purity *because of the power of sexual relationships*. Sex is incredibly important in modern society but, paradoxically, it is also trivialized. One-night stands reduce it to a physical act with no lasting consequences (hopefully). "Safe sex" means sex with a condom, to control health issues. And the Corinthians shared a similar view, especially with a prostitute. What could be less consequential or less significant than a sexual business transaction? But reality is very different. "Shall I then take the members of Christ [my sexual organs] and unite [or join] them with a prostitute? Never! Do you not know that he who unites [joins] himself with a prostitute is one with her in body?" Sexual intercourse, in some powerful way, "joins" and "unites." It is intended for commitment and establishes a unity. It isn't a merely physical act like eating. It is a profoundly personal act. We know, because of sexually transmitted diseases, that one's sexual partners leave a lasting legacy. But Paul is thinking on a much deeper level. Sex outside of permanent commitment still has a permanent effect. But such behavior distorts sexual "union" and diminishes one's self. The "one body" with a prostitute is very different than the "one flesh" intended by God. It is not sexual oneness that is incompatible with our bodies being God's dwelling place, it is sinful sexual encounter.

We are further called to sexual purity *because of the impact of sexual sin.* Paul writes: "All other sins a man commits are outside his body, but he who sins sexually sins against his own body." Commentators have debated the precise meaning of Paul's words and this is not the place to enter into a technical discussion. All sins are serious, and there are sins that have a deep and lasting effect upon our bodies. But sexual sins are not only sins against another, they are self-inflicted wounds that cut to the core of our personhood. Sexual misconduct distorts my relation to Christ, denies the dignity of my body because of my relation to Christ, and diminishes my freedom in Christ. Sexual sins are not necessarily the worst sins, but they are deeply serious sins, which have a profound impact on my self. That is why sexual sin, whether prior to marriage or during marriage, has a devastating affect.

WE NEED TO PURSUE SEXUAL PURITY

The conclusion of Paul is clear: "Flee [literally: make a habit of fleeing] from sexual immorality." If ever this command has relevance, it is in our modern world with its unending opportunities for indulgence. First Thessalonians 4:3 echoes this command: "You should avoid sexual immorality." There are some things God calls us to fight; sexual sin is to be fled. We are to seek safety in flight, sometimes physically, sometimes mentally and emotionally.

First, this means admitting my vulnerability. "If you think you are standing firm, be careful that you don't fall!" (1 Corinthians 10:12). No one is immune. There are things I just don't do, places I will not go, media I dare not see, situations I always avoid. I do not want to dishonor God or devastate my wife by moral failure. The only sure protection is careful self-discipline, and I cannot afford to give myself permission to expose myself to danger. We must honor sexual boundaries established by God.

Second, fleeing immorality means dealing decisively with sinful thoughts, whether pornographic images or romantic fantasies. "Above all else, guard your heart, for it is the wellspring of life" (Proverbs 4:23). "I made a covenant with my eyes not to look lustfully at a girl" (Job 31:1).

Third, fleeing immorality requires seeking help for sinful habits. Habits are not made in a moment and they are rarely broken instantaneously. At the very least, most of us need accountability to keep us on track. Honest admission of my sinful patterns needs to be followed by hard vulnerability to another person of the same sex. Deeply ingrained habits will probably require specific counseling or support-group contexts. But we will not flee immorality if we deny our sinful patterns or apply superficial countermeasures.

Fourth, fleeing immorality means shutting the door on indulgence. There is no greater model than Joseph in Genesis 39:9 as he is enticed by his master's wife: "How then could I do such a wicked thing and sin against God?" Sexual failure is virtually never the result of a momentary lapse. It is the result of indulging sinful thoughts or fantasies. There needs to be a total, heart-level rejection of immorality. At the same time I need to be constantly aware of my responsibility before God and His availability to help me.

But just saying "no" won't cut it. Paul's last command is the most important. "Honor God with your body!" It isn't enough to be good, we need to be good for Someone. A believer is safest when he or she is following hard after God's glory. I honor God with my body not only by avoiding sin but also by enjoying the gift of sex to the full extent within my marriage relationship. His character is revealed and His purpose realized when a husband and wife "become one flesh." Marital sex honors and glorifies God just as surely as premarital celibacy does. That pursuit of "pure pleasure" is the theme of our next two chapters.

Purity takes seriously the glory of God. But it is also important to take seriously the grace of God. We cannot rewrite the past and for some of us, that past includes serious sexual sin. But Christ died for sin and sinners. Real guilt requires real forgiveness, and that is what the cross is all about.

When Hurricane Andrew swept through Florida in 1992, the destruction was incredible. One television crew showed a house standing alone, surrounded by the devastation and debris of its former neighbors. The reporter asked the owner, "Why is yours left when all the rest are gone?" The man's answer was striking: "I built it myself and I built it by the code. When it called for 2' x 6' trusses, I used 2' x 6' trusses; when it called for screws, I used screws. They told me that a house built to code could withstand a hurricane. I did and it did. I guess no one else here followed the code."

God's code of building a house calls for sexual purity. Do it and your marriage will stand even under Hurricane Immorality. Healthy sexuality, exclusive marital intercourse, is truly safe sex.

15

Celebrate the Sexual

ONE OF THE MOST UNCONVENTIONAL LOVE STORIES of our century, celebrated in the movie *Shadowlands*, is the story of C. S. Lewis and Joy Davidman. Lewis was a brilliant, bookish scholar, a lifelong bachelor fifty-eight years old. Joy Davidman was a brash American with a colorful past. Of Jewish birth, Joy had drifted into atheism and Communism until the Lord encountered her and she became a Christ follower. Early in her Christian experience, she was greatly helped by Lewis's writings and began a correspondence with him. Their love of poetry and literature was also a common bond, and when she visited him on a trip to England, they established a friendship.

But Joy's private life was in shambles. Her husband was a womanizing alcoholic and she felt compelled to divorce him. In distress, she sought refuge in England with her two sons, pursued her literary career, and enjoyed her friendship with Lewis. He was strongly attracted to her mind but felt no romantic stirrings toward her, and his friends viewed the relationship with a puzzled bemusement.

This was the Cold War era, however, and in 1956 tensions were at their peak. The British government revoked Joy's resident permit because of her Communist background, and she reluctantly prepared to return to America. This meant facing her husband and battles about the custody of the boys. Lewis was deeply troubled by this. Joy was still emotionally fragile, and turmoil was certain if she returned home. So he made a remarkable offer, on purely compassionate grounds. He would marry Joy so that she could stay in Britain and provide stability for her sons. But it would be only a legal device. They would not live together as husband and wife. So in April, 1956, C. S. Lewis and Joy Davidman were married in a civil ceremony, to satisfy the immigration requirements of the British government.

But life, and the Lord, have a way of surprising us. Joy contracted cancer—terminal cancer. Lewis didn't want her to die alone in a hospital so he committed himself to take her into his house. But he would not do this without doing it honorably before his Lord. So another wedding was arranged—this time a church wedding, so that they would be truly joined in God's eyes.

Two unexpected things took place—Joy's cancer went into remission and Lewis's heart came out of hiding. Their marriage became an exciting, passion-filled relationship that overwhelmed and amazed Lewis. Compassion became passion and concern became intense love. They had only four years together, but the aftermath of her death left him at once devastated by grief and filled with gratitude. As he later wrote:

> For those few years H. and I feasted on love; every mode of it—solemn and merry, romantic and realistic, sometimes as dramatic as a thunderstorm, sometimes as comfortable and unemphatic as putting on your soft slippers. No cranny of heart or body remained unsatisfied. For a good wife contains so many persons in herself. What was H. not to me? She was my daughter and my mother, my pupil and my teacher, my subject and my sovereign; and always, holding all these in solution, my trusty comrade, friend, shipmate, fellow-soldier. My mistress; but at the same time all that any man friend (and I have good ones) has ever been to me. Perhaps more.[1]

Years earlier, Lewis had entitled his spiritual autobiography *Surprised by Joy*. His unusual marriage gave that title an ironic new meaning. God had surprised him with a woman named Joy and the joy of the pleasures they had shared in one another.

God created us for joy. He desires us to experience it, and even the most unlikely marriage, which follows God's Word, can become a source of joy in all its dimensions—spiritual, relational, intellectual, and physical. In fact, sensual joy, a delight in the sexual, is a commanded experience for Christ followers. Far from demeaning or prohibiting the enjoyment of sexuality, God requires it for married couples:

> *Drink water from your own cistern,*
> *running water from your own well.*
> *Should your springs overflow in the streets,*
> *your streams of water in the public squares?*
> *Let them be yours alone,*
> *never to be shared with strangers.*
> *May your fountain be blessed,*
> *and may you rejoice in the wife of your youth.*
> *A loving doe, a graceful deer—*
> *may her breasts satisfy you always,*
> *may you ever be captivated by her love.*
> *Why be captivated, my son, by an adulteress?*
> *Why embrace the bosom of another man's wife?*
> *For a man's ways are in full view of the LORD,*
> *and he examines all his paths.*
> *The evil deeds of a wicked man ensnare him;*
> *the cords of his sin hold him fast.*
> *He will die for lack of discipline,*
> *led astray by his own great folly.*
> (Proverbs 5:15–23)

Few places are more beautiful than Banff National Park in the Canadian Rockies. Tourists journey from all over the world to sightsee, ski, hike, and camp. The vistas are breathtaking, the air is clear, and the water is pure. Or so everyone thought. Early in the 1980s tourists and townspeople began to get very sick. Researchers were amazed to discover that the problem was in the water. It was clear and cold, coming from high up in the mountains, free of human pollution. But a parasite, carried by beavers, had contaminated the water and what became known as "beaver fever" made people extremely ill. It took eleven million dollars and a new water system to solve the problem.

Today the water in Banff is safe. But the episode reminds us that even the purest and most precious things on earth can become contaminated and dangerous. That is also true of our sexuality, as the last chapter indicated. But while impure water is dangerous, pure water is delightful and life giving.

FRESH WATER: SEXUAL PLEASURE IS GOD'S GOOD GIFT

Having grown up in the Pacific Northwest, I took water for granted. Shortage of rainfall was not our problem! Now, having lived for a few years in Southern California, in a climate very similar to that of Israel, my perspective has changed. When water is scarce, life gets much harder. In our modern world, even during a time of drought, water is usually only a faucet away. However, the ancient world had no such conveniences. When drought occurred, life itself was threatened. And when the sun beat down in its fury, running water was precious and delightful. Even today oases such as Jericho and En Gedi are a source of refreshment and beauty in an arid, forbidding landscape.

As the writer of Proverbs addresses his son, he uses water to symbolize our sexuality. What water is to people who live in a semidesert area, sex is to human beings—valuable, refreshing, enjoyable, and life sustaining. Solomon writes from a man's perspective. A man's wife is "your own cistern . . . your own well. . . . your fountain . . . the wife of your youth." His own sexual capacity is a "spring . . . your streams of water." There is a parallel to this in Song of Solomon where the husband says to his bride, "You are a garden fountain, a well of flowing water, streaming down from [the mountains of] Lebanon" (4:15).

The biblical imagery is striking and significant. *Sex is a God-given blessing,* as precious and valuable as pure water. Too often this biblical truth has been covered over by false ideas about the body, by pagan views of sex, or because of reaction to the destructive effect of the misuse of sexuality. Tragically, Christians themselves have often taught totally unbiblical views. Jerome, the great Bible translator, would not allow couples to receive communion after the "bestial" act of intercourse, and he claimed that "he who too ardently loves his own wife is an adulterer." Augustine spoke of "the degrading necessity of sex," and Pope Gregory I claimed that "sexual pleasure can never be without sin." The medieval church suggested abstinence for married couples on Thursday (to honor Christ's arrest); Friday (to honor His crucifixion); Saturday (to honor the virgin Mary); Sunday (to honor Christ's resurrection); and Monday (to honor the departed dead.) That left Tuesday and Wednesday (but not during Lent or Advent). Even Luther felt that he could have found a better way to carry out the procreation of the race. The Victorian era carried this to absurd lengths, leaving the clear impression that sex itself is dirty and unclean. I was brought up in an environment that said little about sex (the less said the better) and never celebrated sexual pleasure as God's gift to His people.

This is a parody of God's truth. Christians must believe in both sexual purity and sexual pleasure. In fact, they believe that sexual purity maximizes sexual pleasure (an idea sustained by modern research polls on sexual satisfaction). Sex can be polluted but it is in itself God's idea, God's good gift, His pure water. There is no more demonic idea than that true discipleship means abandoning sexual delight. The God of Scripture is not the Scrooge of sexual pleasure, nor is Satan its Santa Claus.

Sex has God-given purposes. The primary goal is partnership. The very language of Scripture underlines this. A man and wife "become one flesh," a relationship symbolized and enhanced by sexual union. "Adam knew Eve his wife," we are told in Genesis 4:1, "and she conceived" (KJV). Modern translations tell us that he "had relations" or "lay with" his wife, to clarify the expression. Their substitutes are accurate, but they rob us of a valuable insight. Sex is a way of knowing, of relating, of joining, that transcends the merely physical. It is a way we give up the key to our "selves" in a special way. Physical unity is an aspect of personal intimacy.

Another purpose of sexual union is pleasure and pleasuring. God has created human bodies and our sexual desires in a unique way. We are unlike the animals who are driven by instinct. Our sexual desire is not seasonal. We possess, by creation, sexual organs designed to maximize physical pleasure. The command is to give and receive pleasure: "Rejoice in the wife of your youth."

A third purpose of sex is procreation. God's first command to humans was, "Be fruitful and multiply." This is clearly God's intention. But procreation is not the only or even the most important purpose of sex. God has also created us so that sexual desire and capacity endures long past the capacity for having children. Therefore, those who see sex as having a purely functional purpose (i.e., procreation) have distorted God's intention.

IMPURE WATER: SEXUAL SIN CONTAMINATES MARRIAGE

Water sustains life. But water can be wasted, polluted, or in a time of flood become a source of destruction. The picture in Proverbs warns against letting "your springs overflow in the streets your streams of water in the public square." In context, this can only refer to sexual unfaithfulness. The streets of the ancient world were nearly always hardened dirt or cobblestone. They were filled with animals and their pollution. Water poured out in such streets either vanishes or becomes polluted. Who wants to drink out of a mud puddle? Sexual promiscuity pollutes a precious resource.

Water that has no boundaries sounds like freedom. The truth is, it is either a swamp or a flood. The banks that contain water create the lake or the river. Our society often mocks the restrictiveness of biblical morality. One well-known therapist counsels frustrated couples to engage in "healthy adultery" (the ultimate oxymoron) to rejuvenate their love lives. My mind immediately recalls guilt-ridden, heartbroken people who have broken the banks of their marriage and now weep in my office as they describe the destructive flood they have set loose. We can control our choices; we cannot control the consequences. Helen Gurley Brown, the notorious editor of *Cosmopolitan*, advised (on a network talk show), "I don't think you have to have a raging affair with someone's husband, I'm just saying: Use him, he can do something for you. And that's okay."

No, it isn't. "Using" is not what marriage or personal dignity is all about. That kind of advice is why the warnings of Scripture about marital unfaithfulness are so clear and unequivocal. In Proverbs, because the advice is from a father to a son, the illustrations are about women, but the principles are clearly reciprocal:

> *[Wisdom] will save you also from the adulteress,*
> *from the wayward wife with her seductive words,*
> *who has left the partner of her youth*
> *and ignored the covenant she made before God.*
> *For her house leads down to death*
> *and her paths to the spirits of the dead.*
> *None who go to her return*
> *or attain the paths of life.*
> (Proverbs 2:16–19)

> *For these commands are a lamp,*
> *this teaching is a light,*
> *and the corrections of discipline*
> *are the way to life,*
> *keeping you from the immoral woman,*
> *from the smooth tongue of the wayward wife.*
> *Do not lust in your heart after her beauty*
> *or let her captivate you with her eyes,*
> *for the prostitute reduces you to a loaf of bread,*
> *and the adulteress preys upon your very life.*
> *Can a man scoop fire into his lap*
> *without his clothes being burned?*
> *Can a man walk on hot coals*
> *without his feet being scorched?*
> *So is he who sleeps with another man's wife;*
> *no one who touches her will go unpunished.*
> (Proverbs 6:23–29)

> *"Stolen water is sweet;*
> *food eaten in secret is delicious!"*

> *But little do they know that the dead are there,*
> *that her guests are in the depths of the grave.*
> (Proverbs 9:17–18)

Behind these warnings is a hard-headed realism. There are many things that produce sexual waywardness. It may be personal immaturity one brings into the marriage, unresolved conflicts within the marriage, or unmet needs from the marriage. It may be unchanged habits of the past, or unrealistic expectations about the way it should be. There are a host of reasons why sexual sin becomes desirable.

Nevertheless, sexual unfaithfulness distorts sexuality. Water spilled out is lost forever. It destroys intimacy. I am convinced that casual relationships destroy our capacity for intimacy. Many couples have sentenced themselves to superficial marriages because of premarital habits. Extramarital affairs either devastate trust if they are discovered or lock a door if they are undiscovered. On more than one occasion I have been trapped in a counseling situation that has become very frustrating. One spouse has confessed to me an affair but insisted that I keep it confidential. He or she has then refused to disclose it to the spouse, who is aware that something is terribly wrong but is otherwise in complete darkness. I have suffered with the betrayed partner, who wonders what he or she can do. I've learned to avoid such traps now, but the damage to the marriage and the marriage partner, as well as the children, is enormous. Yet, the reason for the silence is obvious. The sinning partner is deeply aware of the depth of betrayal involved in the sexual sin, and is full of shame or fear. Even worse, some are shameless, with hearts hardened to God and their partners and with eyes closed in denial.

There is another factor that must not be taken lightly. God disciplines believers who engage in sexual sin. He will not allow his children to sin successfully. Sin has God-appointed consequences, as Solomon declares:

> *For a man's ways are in full view of the* LORD,
> *and he examines all his paths.*

The evil deeds of a wicked man ensnare him;
the cord of his sin hold him fast.
He will die for lack of discipline,
led astray by his own great folly.
(Proverbs 5:21–23)

Paul is no less direct: "The Lord will punish men for all such sins, as we have already told you and warned you" (1 Thessalonians 4:6). I remember appealing to a friend who was about to abandon his wife and family for another woman: "Don't do it. I'm afraid for you—of God's discipline of you and of the kind of person you'll become." He has, in years since, paid a hard price. Even worse, he has become a hard man, as he has stubbornly refused to repent under God's chastening hand. His friends, his former wife, his children, his elderly parents have all paid a terrible price, but so has he. He has become an ugly man.

The great need then is preventative maintenance—keeping the streams of marriage clear and between the banks. I need first to affair-proof myself, to keep the dykes of my sexual faithfulness in good repair. I am not exempt from temptation or moral failure. I cannot give myself the luxury of indulging lustful thoughts, toying with flirtatious relationships, or being in vulnerable situations. I cannot visit the sexual chatrooms of the Internet or emotionally engage with another woman. I also need to affair-proof my spouse. Bill Hybels says it well:

> I want to be the kind of husband who will make Lynne stop and say, "I would be crazy to jeopardize what I have." I want her to say, "Why trade a Corvette for a pair of roller skates? Or a Harley for a Honda?" I want to be so devoted to her that the grass all around us looks brown.[2]

Further, I must affair-proof my marriage. People leave if they have little to gain by staying. A weak marriage, a troubled marriage, a devitalized marriage is a very weak magnet. My marriage needs to be a high-investment area, and that specifically involves the sexual side of the relationship. The greener grass doesn't have to be on the other side of the fence!

PURE PLEASURE: GOD'S INVITATION TO SEXUAL PLEASURE

I came to marriage without sexual experience. I can remember the anxiety that came when I read various sexual manuals. Would I ever master these techniques? Would I even remember what I should? Even today, I can be intimidated when I hear people going on about certain feats of sexual athleticism they think are the sine qua non of sexuality. However, thirty years of marriage and pastoral counseling have convinced me that the central principles of sexual pleasure are not issues of technique. I am grateful for Christians who have written biblically, wisely, and sensitively about sexual technique. This is an area in which ignorance is not bliss. But there is more to great sex than great technique. Proverbs directs us to three basic ideas.

First, we are to seek our partner's blessing. "May your fountain be blessed." The command is to bless, not to use or abuse. This means enjoying sex as God intended, in a way that respects and honors my partner. The biblical principle is given in the words of the Lord Jesus: "It is more blessed to give than to receive" (Acts 20:35). In the passage following the one we considered in the previous chapter, Paul writes of marital life:

> *The husband should fulfill his marital duty to his wife, and likewise the wife to her husband. The wife's body does not belong to her alone but also to her husband. In the same way, the husband's body does not belong to him alone but also to his wife. Do not deprive each other except by mutual consent and for a time, so that you may devote yourselves to prayer. Then come together again so that Satan will not tempt you because of your lack of self-control.* (1 Corinthians 7:3–5)

This is not all Scripture says about sex, but it does teach an important truth. There is a mutual marital duty. Sex is not a gift I can choose to give or withhold as I desire. It is an obligation, a duty. God has called me to use my body to bless my partner sexually. In fact, the phrase "do not deprive each other" usually is translated "do not steal or defraud." This is strong language to remind me that I am to accept my responsibility, since marriage involves giving over my body to my partner. But with responsibility goes sensitivity. I have known husbands to demand their sexual rights from their wives on the basis of 1 Corinthians, but to do so in such a way that is using, not blessing. Often women complain about a lack of romance. Men focus on sex rather than love. Men sometimes complain about a lack of responsiveness. That can especially be true if a man fails to come to grips with his wife's fatigue or her unique response system. Sometimes couples use sex as a bartering tool. All of these fall far short of God's intention—sex as a source of blessing and a means of blessing one another.

Second, sexually we are to share mutual delight. "May you rejoice in the wife of your youth." The term *rejoice* is a Hebrew word that says "be glad in, take pleasure in." It is found in a remarkable law God gave to His people in Deuteronomy 24:5: "If a man has recently married, he must not be sent to war or have any other duty laid on him. For one year he is to be free to stay at home and *bring happiness* to the wife he has married." The balance of the command is delightful: God commands a husband "to give pleasure to and to take pleasure in his wife." In both passages, the word has clearly erotic overtones.

This is a radical concept in the ancient world. In other cultures around Israel, as well as in Greece and Rome in New Testament times, marriage was a place of duty, while a man found his pleasure outside marriage, with mistresses or concubines. Even today the idea persists. On television, the vast majority of sexual encounters occur outside marriage and it is assumed that people who delight in sex could never delight in marriage. Monogamy even sounds like monotony. Extramarital sex is enticing, exciting, provocative; marital sex is tedious, boring, and predictable. A number of years ago, Joe Namath embodied the Playboy philosophy in the public eye, while Roger Staubach, the Dallas Cowboy quarterback, was known as a committed family man. During an interview on national television, Phyllis George suddenly asked, "Roger, how do you feel when you compare yourself with Joe Namath, who is so sexually active and has a different woman on his arm every time we see him?" Staubach responded with the cool poise that characterized him as a quarterback: "Phyllis, I'm sure I'm as sexually active as Joe. The difference is that all of mine is with one woman." Great answer. And beyond mere sexual activity stands sexual fulfillment, which is never the payoff from a one-night stand, or a series of compliant partners.

The biblical command is, "Enjoy life with the woman whom you love all the days of your fleeting life which He has given to you under the sun; for this is your reward in life" (Ecclesiastes 9:9 NASB). This mutual delight must deal with three "killer B's"—boredom, busyness, and battering. Boredom is the gradual loss of excitement that comes from taking one another for granted. Busyness produces a loss of intimacy. Battering is emotional or physical abuse. None have any place in God's plan.

Thirdly, we are to pursue pure pleasure. "A loving doe, a graceful deer—may her breasts satisfy you always, may you ever be captivated by her love." The words of Scripture are unblushingly sensual. The words describe sexual satisfaction and sexual intoxication. A husband is commanded to delight in his wife's body, to enjoy its pleasures and to be overwhelmed (the word translated *captivated* means "to be staggered or intoxicated" as in Isaiah 28:7). These are strong words to say that married couples are to enjoy one another sensitively, shamelessly, selflessly, and enthusiastically. Their marriage should be intensely sensual, as they embrace God's gift of sexual enjoyment, found in personal intimacy and sexual understanding. At the same time, their marriage should be intensely spiritual, as they invite the Lord into their sexual experience, receive it as God's gift, and entrust themselves to God's care for His glory.

David Mace has stated it well:

> Married couples who call themselves Christians owe it to one another to take their sex relationships seriously; to give themselves to it wholeheartedly; striving to invest it with all the warmth and richness which it should have, for it is the God given and sacramental expression of their mutual love . . . Far from being a hindrance to the spiritual life [it] should be in every sense an act of worship.[3]

16

Love in Full Bloom

Around the time this book is published, Elizabeth and I will celebrate our thirtieth anniversary. Asking her to marry me was easily the best decision I ever made (apart from my commitment to the Lord Jesus). We have had our share of life's ups and downs, and our journey has involved living in four cities in two countries; raising three wonderful children; making many friends; working together in growing and stimulating ministries; and experiencing grief, loss, and financial reversals. We've been through the storms of hard moves, physical illness, the deaths of all four parents, the pressures of parenting, and the turmoil of ministry. But, through it all, the Lord has deepened and enriched our marriage. As Mark Twain once said, "Love seems the swiftest, but it is the slowest of all growths. No man or woman really know what love is until they have been married a quarter of a century."

Sadly, many couples today will not have the privilege of standing and looking back over decades of shared love. They have opted for another solution to marriage problems which not only robs their children of a united home, it robs them of the privilege of a shared history and a shared future. Elizabeth and I don't have a perfect marriage, but we do have a very rich one, and we have come to treasure what we have.

There are times when we do well to ponder healthy models. One such biblical model is found in an unusual Old Testament book entitled the Song of Solomon. Down through the centuries this book has often been disconcerting to God's people. Some have been troubled by its style. It is poetry and its rich symbolism is difficult, because it takes us into another culture and another window on reality. More have been troubled by its subject matter. The book is sensual, explicit, and erotic, as it describes married life, and highlights the physical part of marriage. Many, more troubled by sex than God is, have been convinced that the book really doesn't mean what it says. It must be an allegory about the soul's relation to God or Israel's union with Yahweh her God, or about the church's connection with Christ, the heavenly bridegroom. I have no doubt that the book can be read in this way but such a superspiritual approach robs us of a basic lesson that God has for us. Others have been troubled by the poem's sexuality. The rabbis suggested young men ought not read it until they reached the age of thirty. I remember vividly the anxious concerns of some when I began to preach through the book several years ago. Songs, they suggested, wasn't really fit for public consumption.

But it is. God is wiser than our inhibitions and it seems strange, in an era as polluted morally as ours, to complain about pure oxygen! The Song of Solomon is, at its clearest intended level of understanding, a love song celebrating the glory of married love. It progresses through the courtship of two lovers (1:1–3:5); celebrates the public and private consummation of the marriage (3:6–5:1), works through a time of conflict and difficulty (5:2–6:13), celebrates the maturity of married love (7:1–8:4), and then looks back in conclusion on the way love works (8:5–14). In this chapter, we want to share in the celebration of mature love and to learn from a healthy model.

A WISE COUPLE CELEBRATES THEIR LOVE

> *How beautiful your sandaled feet,*
> *O prince's daughter!*
> *Your graceful legs are like jewels,*
> *the work of a craftsman's hands.*

Your navel is a rounded goblet
    that never lacks blended wine.
Your waist is a mound of wheat
    encircled by lilies.
Your breasts are like two fawns,
    twins of a gazelle.
Your neck is like an ivory tower.
Your eyes are the pools of Hesbon
    by the gate of Bath Rabbim.
Your nose is like the tower of Lebanon
    looking toward Damascus.
Your head crowns you like Mount Carmel.
Your hair is like royal tapestry;
    the king is held captive by its tresses.
How beautiful you are and how pleasing,
O love, with your delights!
(Song of Songs 7:1–6)

One of the problems in reading an English translation of the Song of Solomon is that we cannot always identify whether the speaker is a man or a woman. However, the Hebrew language makes the gender of the speaker clear, and in these verses the husband is expressing his delight in his wife's beauty. The couple are alone, apparently unclothed, unembarrassed before one another and exuberant about each other. The husband sings a song in praise of his wife's body, beginning with her feet and moving upward, describing her physical features. He had done this before (4:1–7; 5:10–16), but this description is notably more intimate and personal than earlier. As we read it, we notice the obviously poetic and cultural nature of the language. In fact, I always laugh when I read verse 4: "your nose is like the tower of Lebanon." The tower of Lebanon probably refers to a mountain, or a huge rock formation. This woman apparently had quite a nose! Either this man liked big noses or the phrase loses something in translation! But beauty is in the eyes of the beholder. The important thing is that this is the language of love and delight, not the language of manipulation and seduction.

It would be a mistake to pass too quickly over the obvious eroticism of these verses. No wonder the rabbis and the Victorians had trouble with the song! Our culture is no less confused, although in the opposite direction. The marriage bed is pleasing to God. It is pure and to be kept pure (Hebrews 13:4). This then is the language of pure pleasure, God-approved sexual delight, innocent freedom.

The husband is, in fact, expressing an essential ingredient of mature love, *tender affirmation*. Apparently he senses his wife's anxiety about her appearance, as she expressed it in 1:5–6:

> *Dark am I, yet lovely,*
> > *O daughters of Jerusalem,*
> > *dark like the tents of Kedar,*
> > *like the tent curtains of Solomon.*
> *Do not stare at me because I am dark,*
> > *because I am darkened by the sun.*
> *My mother's sons were angry with me*
> > *and made me take care of the vineyards;*
> > *my own vineyard I have neglected.*

Some things don't change very much. Three thousand years ago, this beautiful woman felt insecure about her physical attractiveness. Perhaps even more today, this is a major issue in a culture that values and flaunts physical beauty. Women are made to feel worthwhile or worthless on the basis of appearance, and a husband insensitive to that can bring about lasting damage. This is poignantly revealed in Patty Robert's description of her wedding night, an event that had a toxic effect on the marriage:

> Like most new brides, I had been looking forward eagerly to this night. For the first time in my life, I was going to make love to a man and it was going to be a wonderful thing to do. . . . Richard was going to love me, and maybe that would take this uneasiness out of my heart. Maybe by physically pouring out his love he could take the confusion and fear away from both of us. Maybe we could love it away.

My fantasies were interrupted abruptly when Richard looked up from the bed and said, "You know, you look fatter with your clothes off."

I was devastated. I was self-conscious about my weight anyway. Now I wanted to hide—to cover my nakedness, both physical and emotional—from this man. I did not feel like an adored bride, a precious love object to my husband. I felt fat and unattractive, and I realized with a sinking feeling in the pit of my stomach that while we might make love on this night, we would not be lovers. We might be physically intimate, but there would be no real intimacy between us.

Richard seemed blissfully unaware of the effect his words had produced in me and urged me to come on to bed. I should have shared my feelings with him right then and cleared the air, but I was too hurt. So, I kept silent and we dutifully and rather timidly consummated our marriage.[1]

I find that kind of insensitivity revolting when I see it in someone else. But I have all too many times been insensitive to the damage caused by careless words. A wise husband (and the issue is clearly reciprocal) chooses to nourish and not diminish his wife's confidence. And the physical is only one aspect of that. Bill Farrel provides a much more healthy model:

One day on our honeymoon, I (Pam) had just stepped from the shower and, looking into the mirror, I began to criticize my body. Bill was sitting on the bed, admiring his new wife. As I would comment on an area I thought needed improving, he would counter with how beautiful it was. This went on for a few minutes until he could stand it no longer. He was angry that I would put down his choice of a wife. I was not only tearing myself down but undermining Bill's taste. He stood up, wrapped his arms around me and told me to look straight into his eyes.

I complied, intrigued by the mystery of what my new husband was up to. He very seriously and very lovingly said, "I will be your mirror. My eyes will reflect your beauty. You are beautiful, Pamela. You are perfect, and if you ever doubt it, come stand before me. The mirror of my eyes will tell you the true story. You are perfect for me."

Over the last fourteen years, whenever self-doubt was looming on the horizon, through three pregnancies and baby blues, my mirror has never stopped telling me how perfect I am for him. Because of this continual confidence-building, I have grown more sexually adventurous. In Bill's eyes I am beautiful, and in his arms I am safe.[2]

Coupled with the tender affirmation of the husband is the mutual pleasure of man and wife, as the poem progresses:

> *Your stature is like that of the palm,*
> *   and your breasts like clusters of fruit.*
> *I said, "I will climb the palm tree;*
> *   I will take hold of its fruit."*
> *May your breasts be like the clusters of the vine,*
> *   the fragrance of your breath like apples,*
> *   and your mouth like the best wine.*
> *May the wine go straight to my lover,*
> *   flowing gently over lips and teeth.*
> (Song of Songs 7:7–9)

As he expresses his increasing excitement, he moves from describing his beloved to embracing her. He is obviously sexually aroused, but his delight is not merely in sex but in her. She is not a trophy to be paraded for his ego satisfaction, a plaything for his pleasure, a convenience to be used at his whim, or an object to satisfy his fantasies. There is erotic joy; but it is joy in his wife, not simply from her.

And the bride is neither reticent nor passive. Verse 1 pictures her dancing before him; verse 9 portrays her inviting him to drink of her wine. Truth is distorted by those who say that spiritual women are demure, reserved, and passive sexually. This woman is passionate and assertive. She is a full partner in their sexual yearning and enjoyment. She is playful and unrestrained. Nothing here of Queen Victoria's advice to "lie back and think of England!"

The gift of marriage celebrated in Songs involves mutual pleasure. The man is "[rejoicing] in the wife of [his] youth" (Proverbs 5:18) and she is mirroring that delight. Couples who thrive focus on what they love and enjoy about one another, a mutual delight expressed in sexual delight.

A WISE COUPLE CULTIVATES THEIR LOVE

The words of verses 10–13 are those of the woman. Having interrupted him with her offer of the wine of her love, she continues by declaring her sense of security in their love and inviting him to share in a romantic adventure:

> *I belong to my lover,*
> *and his desire is for me.*
> *Come, my lover, let us go to the countryside,*
> *let us spend the night in the villages.*
> *Let us go early to the vineyards*
> *to see if the vines have budded,*
> *if their blossoms have opened,*
> *and if the pomegranates are in bloom—*
> *there I will give you my love.*
> *The mandrakes send out their fragrance,*
> *and at our door is every delicacy,*
> *both new and old,*
> *that I have stored up for you, my lover.*
> (Song of Songs 7:10–13)

One of the greatest gifts a partner can give his or her spouse is a sense of confidence, of being loved and valued. The bride delights in this gift: "I am my lover's and his desire is for me." This is the third time she has expressed such an idea, and the progression in her sense of confidence is striking. The first occasion she exults, "My lover is mine and I am his" (2:16). They share a reciprocal love. The second occasion reverses the order: "I am my lover's and my lover is mine." But now she rejoices: "I belong to my lover, and his desire is for me" (7:10). The word *desire* is fascinating. It is used elsewhere only in a context we have previously visited—Genesis 3:16, where the woman's desire is for her husband. Here the situation is reversed, and the woman is the object of her husband's desire. In this relationship of mutual delight and loving enjoyment it is almost as if the fall has been reversed.

There is a sense in which that is true. We are never quite as close to Eden as in those moments where the purity of love removes the fig leaves and the two, naked and unashamed, become one flesh. The gift of security and acceptance, a knowing that we can safely trust and desire one another, is a special gift. It means that sexual desire has become love, rather than lust. Stephen Arterburn describes the difference:

> Love is personal; lust is impersonal. Love is concrete, focused on a particular object; lust is unfocused, capable of fixing on almost any available object. Love tends toward faithfulness; lust is a wanderer. Love seeks stability; lust is short-lived and mercurial. Love is an affair of the mind and heart; lust is an affair of the emotions and hormones. Love is a matter of giving; lust is a matter of taking.[3]

In her confidence in her husband's love, the woman is free to express her desire for him. She invites her husband to a romantic adventure, full of enjoyment and sexual anticipation. Once again, the absence of reticence and feminine inhibition is evident. It is possible to read too much of our modern world into this poem, but this wise woman seems to recognize the need to escape the routines of life with their distractions and exhaustion.

Many marriages falter not because of sexual waywardness but because of persistent busyness. The incessant demands of modern life chip away at our relationships subtly but certainly. A thriving marriage requires a mutual commitment of time and creativity to keep romance and passion alive. Neglect and selfishness slowly strangle intimacy. Therefore, we need to work together to maintain a sense of spontaneity, adventure, and seductiveness. Special times, special places, special activities are not an expense so much as an investment in the future. I am astonished when I hear couples complain that they cannot afford such times. First, budget-wise people don't need to spend very much money. Creativity is more valuable than luxury. Second, the cost of not doing this may become staggeringly high, both financially and emotionally.

A WISE COUPLE "CLOSES" THEIR LOVE

The third stanza of the poem presents the lovers in another mood. The bride expresses her desire for intimacy with her husband in terms that seem rather strange to us:

> *If only you were to me like a brother,*
> *who was nursed at my mother's breasts!*
> *Then, if I found you outside,*
> *I would kiss you,*
> *and no one would despise me.*
> *I would lead you*
> *and bring you to my mother's house—*
> *she who has taught me.*
> *I would give you spiced wine to drink,*
> *the nectar of my pomegranates.*
> *His left arm is under my head*
> *and his right arm embraces me.*
> (Song of Songs 8:1–3)

Why would this bride long for a brother-sister relationship with her husband? That is not what she is desiring. In the world of the Songs, public contact between members of the opposite sex, even marriage partners, was severely limited. Only a harlot would take hold of him and kiss him publicly (Proverbs 7:13). But no such restrictions were placed upon family members. They could touch and kiss freely and openly. She longs to express her love in uninhibited ways in every area of life. And perhaps her words express a desire, like many lovers know, to have known the lover since childhood, to have shared a rich heritage of memories.

Her desire is for intimacy, expressed physically but experienced at a much deeper level. Intimacy is achieved through long-term sharing of the soul. I have known Elizabeth for more than thirty years. But time alone does not produce intimacy. Intriguingly, the bride suggests that there is an art to love and intimacy that she learned from her mother. Moreover in verse three she repeats a phrase that she has used before, in 2:6: "His left arm is under my head and his right arm embraces me."

This is an embrace of love and closeness that they have shared before.

Cliff and Joyce Penner have written some of the most helpful books on a healthy Christian view and experience of sex. They clearly understand its importance.:

> How important is sex in a marriage? A simple answer is that, when marriage is compared with an automobile, sex is to the marriage what oil is to the combustion engine. At least a little oil is necessary to keep the engine running—without sex, one's marriage engine will eventually break down.
>
> Even though the sexual dimension needs to be taken very seriously, it must be kept in proper perspective. Sex is not everything! The oil level of the car might be just fine, but without fuel and a full complement of working parts, the car just sits there. So what is the fuel in a marriage?
>
> Intimacy! Everything that makes a marriage run smoothly falls under the category of intimacy: communication, interests, activities, finances, spiritual connection, parenting, household management, social life, and of course, sex. Intimacy, in the context of a lifelong commitment, sets the marriage apart from all other relationships. A marriage without intimacy is like a car that is resting up on blocks in the back yard. It is a car, but it no longer serves the function for which it was designed. A marriage without intimacy is technically still a marriage, but it does not fulfill its original purpose.[4]

The couple in the Songs have sought the treasure of intimacy in their relationship. The final verse of the section repeats a refrain heard in 2:7 and 3:5, a warning that calls us to understand that a healthy marriage needs the closure of purity, a shutting of the door on all relationships outside marriage:

> *Daughters of Jerusalem, I charge you:*
> > *Do not arouse or awaken love*
> *until it so desires.*
> (Song of Songs 8:4)

The tone of this statement is emphatic in Hebrew: "never arouse and never awaken love." It is a warning against premature or inappropriate sexual desire. The last part of the phrase needs to be considered carefully. "Do not arouse or awaken love until it is right." The NIV translation, "until it so desires," is not very helpful. Love is always ready to be aroused—that's the problem. But there is a right time and a right context to express sexual love. In the full enjoyment of sexual love, the woman throws out a caution: Await God's time. Protect your purity. Express sexual love only within marriage.

This is not an afterthought, and in the context of Songs it is clearly not motivated by a fear of sexual pleasure. The opposite is true. Untimely sexual involvement hinders the ability to find freedom in marriage. That is true even when a couple are fully committed to marriage. I have dealt scores of times with couples who face serious problems in their marriage because they engaged in sexual relations with one another prior to marriage. We enhance pleasure by purity. A *Wall Street Journal* report indicated that it is morally strict couples who report the highest sexual pleasure. That is hardly the message of the media but it is the truth of God. In fact, sexual waywardness destroys the capacity both for intimacy and for ecstasy.

The Song of Songs is a poem that celebrates the love of a young woman and her husband. It moves from the first pleasures of love to the rich experience of a mature and tested love. It confronts our jaded world, with its decadent morals, perverted tastes, and pornographic seductions, with a view of innocent delight and pure sensuality that it can barely understand. But Songs is not given to us simply as a remarkable work of artistry. It is a portrait of the garden of delights. God wants married couples to enter the garden characterized by tender affirmation, mutual pleasure, security, creativity, intimacy, and purity. There is a garden of physical pleasures the Lord wants us to experience, as we pursue His wholeness in a world whose sexual garden is overgrown with toxic weeds and filled with destructive animals.

17

Rekindling the Spark

A N OLD MAN, LYING ON HIS DEATHBED, became aware through the haze of medication that his wife of fifty-five years was sitting beside his bed. "Oh, it's you, Ethel, at my side once again."

"Yes, dear."

"Do you remember when Uncle Sam sent my draft notice after Pearl Harbor? You were with me then. And when I was in the Veteran's Hospital, you were with me then. You were there when that truck smashed our very first car that we'd saved so hard for. And when our house burned to the ground and we lost everything. And, Ethel, when our little shop went under and we were flat broke—you were at my side then."

"Yes, dear."

He gave a deep sigh. "I tell you, Ethel. You're bad luck!"

Longevity is a great accomplishment in a day when many marriages don't survive very long. But durability, while admirable, is not adequate. A marriage needs to do more than endure. It needs to grow and mature. Time alone will not strengthen a marriage. There is an old story of a teacher who complained, after being passed over for promotion, "After all, I have twenty years experience." "No," his supervisor said. "You have one year of experience repeated twenty times." The quality of our experience is far more important than merely quantity.

After thirty years of marriage, Elizabeth and I don't have a perfect love. But we do have a rich love, by God's grace, and we are committed to seeing it become richer. We haven't acquired this richness automatically, and we haven't reached coasting speed. We are committed to this basic truth: *no matter how successful a relationship appears, it is in need of continual renewal and refreshment.* We are committed to finishing well. That means we continually need to modify our course to stay on target. Complacency breeds failure. If we are not careful, we will end up where we never intended. We need to keep our relationship fresh and to make sure, when our relationship with the Lord and one another becomes stale or static, that we take immediate corrective measures.

The church of Ephesus in New Testament times was already a church with a remarkable past. But its actual condition was very different from its reputation and heritage. It was a church in trouble, with unseen decay. The Lord's prescription for this church is a helpful paradigm for rekindling the spark in our essential relationships:

> "To the angel of the church in Ephesus write:
> These are the words of him who holds the seven stars in his right hand and walks among the seven golden lampstands: I know your deeds, your hard work and your perseverance. I know that you cannot tolerate wicked men, that you have tested those who claim to be apostles but are not, and have found them false. You have persevered and have endured hardships for my name, and have not grown weary.
> Yet I hold this against you: You have forsaken your first love. Remember the height from which you have fallen! Repent and do the things you did at first. If you do not repent, I will come to you and remove your lampstand from its place. But you have this in your favor: You hate the practices of the Nicolaitans, which I also hate.

> *He who has an ear, let him hear what the Spirit says to*
> *the churches. To him who overcomes, I will give the right to*
> *eat from the tree of life, which is in the paradise of God."*
> (Revelation 2:1–7)

Before Ross Perot became known as a political spokesman, he had established a reputation as a creative and successful businessman. His words about business are equally relevant to other areas: "Every good and excellent thing stands moment by moment on the razor's edge of danger and must be fought for." The Ephesians had ignored that. They had been a state-of-the-art church, the most effective church described in the New Testament. But a subtle process was at work and it was eating the heart out of the church. That same process affects marriage, so we need to listen to the Lord's evaluation.

WE NEED TO RECOGNIZE OUR STRENGTHS

The Lord does not begin by exposing the Ephesian church's problems. He first reminds them that they have a track record of success. The name of Ephesus represented success, both for the city and the congregation. The city itself was prominent, the first and most important city of the ancient Roman province of Asia. It was located three miles up the Cayster River and it was a major port and training center. The population was large for a city of that time, about a third of a million, and it had a reputation as a city of beauty and culture. Its architecture was famous, especially the temple of the goddess Artemis (or Diana), one of the seven wonders of the world. Its commerce was prosperous, its religion was powerful although pagan, its culture was influential.

The church in Ephesus was one of God's wonders. Founded under the ministries of Apollos and Paul, it had flourished, planting daughter churches throughout the entire region. "All the Jews and Greeks who lived in the province of Asia heard the word of the Lord" (Acts 19:10), as it radiated out from Ephesus. Significant people had served as leaders—people such as Timothy, Aquila and Priscilla, Tychicus, and the apostle John. More books of the New

Testament were written to Ephesus than to any other church. Obviously, then, the Ephesian church was an important, healthy, effective, spiritually affluent church, and the Lord's appraisal reflects its genuine strengths.

The messages of the Lord Jesus to the seven churches of Asia found in Revelation 2 and 3 follow a common pattern. The Savior begins with a description of Himself, followed by an affirmation of each church's strengths. He then puts His finger on an issue in the church's life that requires repentance and correction, and concludes with a promise for those who respond in obedience.

The Lord introduces himself to the Ephesian believers as the One who "holds the seven stars in his hand" ("stars" are identified as the "angels of the churches" in Revelation 1:20) and "walks among the seven golden lampstands" (Revelation 2:1—a lampstand symbolizes a local church). The Lord wants us to know that He controls (or holds) His church and patrols (by walking among) His church. He is not remote and removed from our lives. He is intimately acquainted with us. He does not view our churches or our marriages from afar.

And what He sees pleases Him. The words that describe the Ephesians are very positive. They are characterized by active ministry ("I know your deeds, your hard work and your perseverance"), doctrinal purity ("I know that you cannot tolerate wicked men . . . and have found them false"); and personal integrity ("you have persevered and have endured hardships"). If the description ended at verse three, the Ephesians could have used the slogan: "we do church right." These are not trivial matters. The Ephesian church was strong, precisely where a church needs to be strong.

Our marriages can be like that. Almost every marriage has strengths, things a couple does well. Wise Christian couples know their relational strengths and build upon them. The Lord does not begin by focusing on weaknesses and neither should we. I have found it useful to distinguish strengths, weaknesses, and sins. Strengths are assets, positive areas; weaknesses are abilities we do not possess or capacities we do not have or have not developed; sins are sins, issues that require repentance and change. Wise couples build on their strengths, learn to manage their weaknesses and keep them under control, and honestly admit and vigorously deal with sins. That was precisely the problem at Ephesus. Whether or not they appreciated their strengths, they did not recognize that they had a fatal lack, which threatened their very existence, a lack which was not merely a weakness but a sin.

WE NEED TO REASSESS OUR "SUCCESS"

The city of Ephesus was in the midst of a crisis it did not recognize. Slowly but surely, the harbor was filling with silt and the river was becoming a swamp, not a stream. The very port that was its basis of existence and its source of prosperity was going out of existence. I don't know what kind of technology the first century had available to deal with such a problem. I do know that its first-century glory was an illusion. As the harbor became more and more clogged, a process unseen beneath the smooth surface of its waters, Ephesus was becoming less and less viable as a port. Today all that remains is ruins, and they are eight miles upstream. Ephesus is no longer a seaport city.

The risen Christ diagnoses the same condition in the Ephesian church. Its spiritual arteries are becoming clogged and a life-threatening heart condition is setting in. There are no visible external signs of distress. Onlookers see only a successful, thriving church. But the Lord of the church pierces beneath the visible: "I hold this against you: you have forsaken your first love. . . . Repent." The distinguishing mark of a believer is faith working through love—a love for God which results in a love for His people. The two are intertwined, since "anyone who does not love his brother, whom he has seen, cannot love God, whom he has not seen. . . . Whoever loves God must also love his brother" (1 John 4:20–21).

I doubt that the Lord is complaining that the Ephesians have lost the emotional rush, the infatuated feelings that accompany the early days of a romance, whether spiritual or romantic. First love is not an issue of time so much as priority. Paul speaks in 2 Corinthians 11:3 about the danger of being "led astray from your sincere and pure devotion to Christ." First love is a fresh, free, flexible commitment that values the Lord Jesus above all else. And it isn't that they have *lost* this love. They have *left* it. This is not the accident of circumstances but the product of choices. This is not a inevitable result, but an avoidable condition.

The Lord's words should cause every Christian to do some serious self-analysis about his or her spiritual life. This is not a trivial issue. The Lord clearly says that He would rather have no church at all rather than a loveless one: "If you do not repent, I will come to you and remove your lampstand from its place" (Revelation 2:5). No catalog of virtues can compensate for the absence of love. And it should be noted that the Ephesians had not fallen into overt moral sin. They had left their first love. That is not merely an unfortunate state of affairs. It is an extremely serious sin that requires repentance. A church that is orthodox and active but loveless is a spiritual machine; it is not the body of Christ.

A missionary in east Africa reported an interesting phenomenon. He noticed that groups of Africans would walk past government hospitals and travel many extra miles to receive treatment at a mission hospital. When he asked why they would walk so much farther when the same treatment was much more conveniently available at the government clinic, their answer was: "The medicines may be the same but the hands are different." Love is not a small difference. It is all the difference in the world.

Likewise, a marriage can be outwardly successful and apparently healthy, but inwardly barren. Every marriage inevitably goes through various stages, and the seasons of life affect marriage deeply. The marital enthusiasm of the honeymoon stage must move into the stage of marital adjustment to the realities of living with one another and balancing the demands of life. Change is inevitable; atrophy is avoidable. But life is difficult. Problems have a way of silting up the stream of marriage—the demands of career, the presence of children, the pressure of money, the changes of life, the accumulated baggage of the past, the anxieties of living. These occur, but marital fulfillment comes when we cling hard to our first love. "Silt" is inevitable; wise couples know that only continual dredging will keep the harbor clear.

There are various ways to detect a leaving of first love. One is a loss of enthusiasm, a personal complacency that begins to settle for the status quo. A want ad captures the painful reality of this in a humorous way:

> For Sale: one 52-year-old husband. Never remembers anniversaries, birthdays, or special days. Seldom holds hands, hugs, kisses, or says "I love you!" Rarely is kind or tender. Will sell cheap—two cents. Call 555-0366. Will dicker.

Sheldon Vanauken expresses the same idea in other terms:

> The killer of love is creeping separateness—taking love for granted, especially after marriage. Finding separate interests. "We" turning into "I." Self. Self-regard: what I want to do. . . . The failure of love might seem to be caused by hate or boredom or unfaithfulness with a love, but those were results. First came the creeping separateness, the failure behind the failure.[1]

Lewis Smedes portrays another picture of a devitalized marriage:

> A man or woman can be just too busy, too tired, too timid, too prudent, or too hemmed in with fear to be seriously tempted by an adulterous affair. But this same person can be a bore at home, callous to the delicate needs of his partner. He or she may be too prudish to be an adventuresome lover, but too cowardly to be in honest communication and too busy to put himself out for anything more than a routine ritual of personal commitment. He/she may be able to claim that he/she never cheated; but he/she may never have tried to grow along with his/her partner into a deep, personal relationship of respect and regard within marriage. His/her brand of negative fidelity may be an excuse for letting the marriage fall by neglect into dreary conformity to habit and, with that, into dull routine of depersonalized sex. I am not minimizing the importance of negative fidelity; but anyone who thinks that morality in marriage is fulfilled by avoiding an affair with a third party has short-circuited the personal dynamics of fidelity."[2]

The question is an urgent one: How would the Lord evaluate your marriage? We can, like the Ephesians, mislead others about what is going on under the surface. But this divine stethoscope reads what others can't see. How is your heart? Is there "first love" or have you left that behind? The measure of a marriage isn't the size of your house or the quality of your lifestyle but the hunger of your heart. Love is a set of actions and attitudes that exalts the needs of another. It involves an emotional climate of loving and nurturing, a servant attitude of partnering and ministering, a spiritual bond of trusting the living God.

An old saying advises: "if it ain't broke, don't fix it." Reality is very different. If you don't fix it all the time, it will break. Tony Gwynn is one of baseball's greatest hitters, who has consistently led the National League in hitting. The reason is found in his philosophy: "I don't think I'll ever be satisfied. Once you think you're where you want to be, you're not there anymore." Wise couples know the same thing. If we plateau, we plunge. If we don't pay attention, the harbor silts. If we don't keep it fresh, it goes stale.

Every marriage needs either rekindling or refreshing. There are no exceptions. External impressiveness is no substitute for internal authenticity. And the Lord gives us a handle on the process in His counsel to the Ephesians.

WE CONTINUALLY NEED TO "RE-PAIR" OUR RELATIONSHIPS

There are three specific commands which the Lord gives to the Ephesians to help them deal with their forsaken first love: "Remember . . . repent . . . do the things you did at first [repeat]." These are not only the three essential steps of spiritual renewal, they are the steps necessary to rekindle a marriage relationship.

"Remember": Recapturing Your Vision

The Cayster River in Ephesus did not silt up overnight. There was an inexorable process at work that was slowly but steadily clogging the stream. The Ephesian church did not lose its spiritual vitality all at once. There were a series of choices that led them further and further from their first love. Marriages rarely suffer catastrophic failure, like an unexpected car crash. Heart failure occurs over time, although the crisis may occur in a moment of time. We form habits that are destructive, but their danger is not immediately obvious. Lack of communication, unresolved conflicts, neglected intimacy, petty discourtesies and disrespects, complacency, pervasive criticism—habits form channels in our relationships, the ruts of least resistance. It becomes easier to stay where we are than to exert the energy to break out.

That is why a couple needs careful remembrance—a conscious calling to mind of the good times, the special memories, the appreciated strengths, the positive builders of a relationship. What made our relationship good? I have never counseled a couple prior to marriage who could not enthusiastically describe one another's strengths and the strengths of their relationship. But when a marriage is in crisis, the same couple often have very little ability to remember those very attributes that once seemed so clear. We allow the negatives to totally obscure our shared assets.

The purpose of remembering is not nostalgia about "the way we were." The need is to establish benchmarks by which to evaluate the present and to recapture a vision for the future. We cannot solve problems we do not or will not see. Remembering our strengths and moments of glory removes the fog of the present. First love is a time of discovering one another—too often in the present we fail to accept one another. First love is a time of focusing attention on the other. Are we taking one another for granted? First love is a time of making time for one another and seeking to please one another. Have we drifted into our own separate worlds?

Elizabeth and I delight to talk about the special times of the past. We don't want to live there—we're much more interested in the future. But the strengths of our past are the foundation of our future. And there are times when Elizabeth has reminded me of a special time of intimacy back then, and graciously encouraged me to realize that my present pattern of behavior is defeating the possibility of repeating that. "Remember the height from which you have fallen!"—not to assign blame or to lament the present.

We remember so that we can unbury our dreams and rekindle or refresh our relationship.

"Repent": Renew Your Commitment

I am struck by this command. Lovelessness is not just sad, it is sin. Marriages fail or flounder because of the hardness of human hearts, and marital failure is rarely one-sided. The essential requirement for renewal is an honest admission of one's shortcomings and a genuine acceptance of personal responsibility.

Repentance lies at the very heart of the Christian faith. People who meet the living God change the way they see themselves and the way they see God. Repentance goes far deeper than regret. It is a return to reality about ourselves, a stripping away of denial, blaming, or rationalization. It is an honest, heartfelt acknowledgment of failure before God first, and then before my partner. There is nothing superficial about genuine repentance. It is incredibly painful, but it is also wonderfully purifying.

I remember a particularly difficult marriage breakdown. These were friends of mine, people who had been very kind to us. But now they were caught in an avalanche of mutual recriminations, wounding words, and deep attacks. The rule if you are caught in an avalanche is to swim with the flow to try to reach the surface. There was a moment—I remember it vividly—of incredible power in our counseling. The Lord had broken in, deeply reached into those two people's hearts, and a golden moment had arrived. I knew that they would surface into clear air if either would have the courage to say: "I'm sorry. I was wrong. Please forgive me. I forgive you." It was awfully quiet. But neither would do it, they fought against God's moving, the moment passed, and an avalanche of bitterness and hatred swept them away. That marriage died soon after.

A study of almost two hundred top-level executives in Fortune 500 companies revealed that nearly all of them had suffered setback experiences in their business careers, experiences ranging from failure to firing. The survey showed that executives who bounced back did so because, instead of blaming others, they were able to admit their mistakes, learn from them, and move on. Repentance involves more than admission. It involves applying the extra energy to break out of the rut of habit. A plane uses most of its fuel on take-off, to overcome the pull of gravity. The gravity of the status quo holds us down. Repentance is an energy-demanding jet thrust out of the status quo. It is hard work and many are unwilling to pay the price. All too often men ignore the warning signals from their wives, when change would be relatively painless. When they finally get the message, the effort required to change is overwhelming. Therefore wise couples are good repenters. They don't save it up; they do it now.

"Repeat": Reclaim Lost Ground

The Lord's third command is a striking one. He does not say to people who have left their first love: "feel your first feelings." The command is "do the things you did at first." The need is consciously to choose to do the things that love requires, however your emotions complain. Love is not primarily a slave of our emotions, it is a servant of our wills. We are to do what is loving. We act in love, so that we may feel love.

It is amazing, as I think back, how many "wise" things I did when I first fell in love with Elizabeth, even though I was very foolish and immature. I listened to her, spent time with her, complimented her, went out of my way to let her know she was special to me. I arranged special times, went special places, bought special gifts. I talked to her, told her about myself, shared my hopes and feelings. I took her to romantic places and tried to create romantic moments. I'm not saying these things to compliment myself. I didn't do them because I was smart, I did them because I was in love. It took a lot of energy, but I don't remember ever thinking about that. It didn't take much money because I didn't have any. And when I hurt her or something came between us, I wanted to put that right at the first possible moment.

And what keeps my marriage fresh today is repeating those first things. To the extent that I neglect them, I allow the harbor to silt. To the extent that I continue the courtship experience, I keep my first love.

Some who read these words will experience an enormous fear of reengagement. What if it doesn't work? What if he or she doesn't respond? The fear is real, but it is also irrelevant. One who has left his or her first love is not pleasing the Lord. The first step may be to renew that primary love relationship: to do some deep spiritual connecting with the Good Shepherd. But the time must come when, for the glory of God and for the good of all concerned, one must step out in obedience to God to remember, repent, and repeat. Hopefully, complete reconciliation will result. But God wills us to obey and not to wait.

Conclusion

When I was a boy I read an adventure story that left me aware of the poisonous bite of the black widow spider. Since no such creatures existed in my part of Canada, my interest was entirely theoretical. But why was it called a widow spider? The encyclopedia's answer fascinated me: "The male is seldom seen because it is often killed and eaten by the female after mating." I later discovered the praying mantis has the same habit. Imagine how it might feel to be one of those hapless male insects, hungry for a little love and affection, only to discover that not only are you on the love menu, you are the lunch menu!

With regard to the human species, neither gender has a monopoly on devouring the other. But the pattern is far too common. We enter marriage to enjoy, develop, and experience intimacy with one another. But along the way, things begin to go wrong and we end up biting and even devouring one another.

God's intention is very different. Peter states it beautifully in 1 Peter 3. Having described the way husbands and wives are to follow the example of Christ in their relations with one another, he summarizes God's intention for all our relationships, especially marriage, in verses 8 and 9:

> *Finally, all of you, live in harmony with one another; be sympathetic, love as brothers, be compassionate and humble. Do not repay evil with evil or insult with insult, but with blessing, because to this you were called so that you may inherit a blessing.*

Marriage can be either a battleground or a blessing. God's intention is clear: we are divinely called to inherit a blessing. But this is not automatic. We inherit a blessing by choosing to be a blessing. To bless another means, at its most basic level, to speak well of him or her. At its most important level, it means to invoke God's favor and to desire God's best for one's partner.

One of God's greatest promises was made to Abraham. Called the Abrahamic covenant, it contains a promise that shapes human history.

> *I will make you into a great nation*
> *and I will bless you;*
> *I will make your name great*
> *and you will be a blessing.*
> *I will bless those who bless you,*
> *and whoever curses you I will curse;*
> *and all people on earth*
> *will be blessed through you.*
> (Genesis 12:2–3)

Someone has perceptively observed that Israel's greatest mistake, in the light of God's covenant, was that she was more concerned about getting a blessing than being a blessing. And so she turned in on herself and failed to accomplish God's purposes for her. As a result, she squandered the blessing.

In a sense, that is the theme of this book. God gave marriage as a blessing. He has called us to inherit a blessing. But God's process is unchanging. We get a blessing only as we become a blessing. This theme runs throughout God's Word as an immutable law of life: "Whoever tries to keep his life will lose it, and whoever loses his life will preserve it" (Luke 17:33; see Luke 9:24 and John 12:24–26). As we have seen over and over, the greatest killer of marriage is justified self-centeredness; the great model for marriage is the cross of Christ. The narrow road of obedience to Christ is the only road that leads to life and blessing.

Christ followers take marriage seriously, because their Lord does. Christ followers embrace marriage enthusiastically, because they receive it as the gift of a gracious God who calls us to inherit a blessing. Christ followers invest in marriage lavishly, because they know it is the work of a lifetime. Christ followers build a marriage wisely, because they value supremely the instructions of an all-wise God.

May your marriage become a blessing to you and to a needy world around you as you give a blessing to your partner.

Endnotes

CHAPTER ONE

1. Peggy Noonan, *Life, Liberty and the Pursuit of Happiness* (Holbrook, MA: Adams Publishing, 1994), 36.
2. David Mace, "Strictly Personal," *Marriage and Family Living*, November 1980 (62:11), 2.

CHAPTER TWO

1. Daniel Goleman, *Emotional Intelligence* (New York: Bantam, 1995), 179, italics orig.

CHAPTER THREE

1. Cited in H. Norman Wright, *More Communication Keys to Your Marriage* (Glendale, CA: Regal, 1983), 15–16.
2. Larry Crabb, *Men and Women: Enjoying the Difference* (Grand Rapids, MI: Zondervan, 1991), 28.

CHAPTER FOUR

1. "I Do, I Do—for Now," *Los Angeles Times,* 28 November 1994, E3.
2. Mike Mason, *The Mystery of Marriage* (Sisters, OR: Multnomah, 1985), 94.
3. Robert Roberts, *Taking the Word to Heart* (Grand Rapids, MI: Eerdmans, 1993), 207–8.
4. Jeff Van Vonderen, *Families Where Grace Is in Place* (Minneapolis: Bethany House, 1992), 151.
5. David Myers, *The Pursuit of Happiness* (New York: William Morrow, 1992), 162.
6. Lewis Smedes, *Caring and Commitment* (Grand Rapids, MI: Eerdmans, 1989), 23.
7. Wayne House, editor, *Divorce and Remarriage: Four Christian Views* (Downers Grove, IL: InterVarsity Press, 1990).
8. Robertson McQuilkin, "Living by Vows," *Christianity Today*, 8 October 1990, 38–40.

CHAPTER FIVE

1. Jerry Lewis, *How's Your Family?* (New York: Brunner/Mazel, 1979), 21.

2. Karl Hess, "Serve," in Colin Brown, editor, *The New International Dictionary of New Testament Theology* (Grand Rapids, MI: Zondervan, 1971), 3:544.

3. Gary Chapman, *The Five Love Languages: How to Express Heartfelt Commitment to Your Mate* (Chicago: Northfield, 1994).

4. Jeff Van Vonderen, *Families Where Grace Is in Place* (Minneapolis: Bethany House, 1992).

5. Adapted from a message delivered at "The Church in the Twentieth-Century" Conference, Orlando, Florida, 28 June 1993.

CHAPTER SIX

1. Bruce Larson, *No Longer Strangers* (Waco, TX: Word Books, 1971), 136.

2. Deborah Tannen, *You Just Don't Understand* (New York: Ballantine Books, 1990).

3. David Augsburger, *The Freedom of Forgiveness* (Chicago: Moody Press, 1970), 86.

CHAPTER SEVEN

1. John Gottman, *Why Marriages Succeed or Fail* (New York: Simon and Schuster, 1994), 139.

2. Gottman, 28.

3. Gottman, 57.

4. David Myers, *The Pursuit of Happiness* (New York: William Morrow, 1992), 172.

5. Carol Travis, *Psychology Today*, November 1982.

6. Margery Williams, *The Velveteen Rabbit* (New York: Avon Books, 1975), 13.

CHAPTER EIGHT

1. Sandra Wilson, *Hurt People Hurt People* (Nashville, TN: Thomas Nelson, 1993).

2. Sandra Wilson, *Released from Shame* (Downer's Grove, IL: Inter-Varsity Press, 1990), 141.

CHAPTER NINE

1. James Oliver Buswell, *A Systematic Theology of the Christian Religion* (Grand Rapids, MI: Zondervan, 1963), 2:131.

2. C. S. Lewis, *Fern Seed and Elephants,* ed. Walter Hooper (Glasgow:

Fontana/Collins, 1975), 42.

3. Frederick Buechner, *Wishful Thinking: A Theological ABC* (New York: Harper and Row, 1973), 2.

CHAPTER TEN

1. Robert Bly, *Iron John* (Reading, MA: Addison-Wesley, 1990), 2–3.
2. Bly, 150–51.
3. Dorothy Sayers, *Are Women Human?* (Downer's Grove, IL: Inter-Varsity Press, 1971), 47.
4. For more on biblical friendship, see my book *Quality Friendship* (Chicago: Moody Press, 1981).

CHAPTER ELEVEN

1. Pierre Mornell, *Passive Men; Wild Women* (New York: Ballantine Books, 1980), 1–2.
2. John Piper, *Recovering Biblical Manhood and Womanhood* (Wheaton, IL: Crossway Books, 1991), 39.
3. William Barclay, *The Letters to the Galatians and Ephesians*, *The Daily Study Bible* (Edinburgh: The Saint Andrew Press, 1958), 199–203.
4. Cited in Jack Balswick and Judith Balswick, *The Family: A Christian Perspective on the Contemporary Home* (Grand Rapids, MI: Baker, 1990), 165.

CHAPTER TWELVE

1. Carol Gilligan, *In a Different Voice* (Cambridge, MA: Harvard University Press, 1982), 159–60.
2. Gail MacDonald, *Keep Climbing* (Wheaton, IL: Tyndale House, 1989), 42.
3. Cited by MacDonald, 52.
4. *Prime Time*, July 1, 1993.
5. Hans Selye, quoted by Stephen Covey, A. Roger Merrill and Rebecca R. Merrill, *First Things First* (New York: Simon and Schuster, 1994), 200.

CHAPTER THIRTEEN

1. Mike Mason, *The Mystery of Marriage* (Sisters, OR: Multnomah, 1985), 139.
2. Gerhard Delling, in Gerhard Kittl and Gerhard Friedrich, ed., *Theological Dictionary of the New Testament* (Grand Rapids, MI: Eerdmans, 1972), 8:45.

3. Markus Barth, *Ephesians 4–6, The Anchor Bible* (Garden City, NY: 1960), 609, 710.
4. C. B. Cranfield, *I and II Peter and Jude, Torch Bible Commentaries* (London: SCM Press, 1960), 74–75.
5. J. C. Pollock, *Hudson Taylor and Maria* (New York: McGraw-Hill, 1962), 172.

CHAPTER FIFTEEN

1. C. S. Lewis, *A Grief Observed* (Toronto: Bantam Books, 1926), 6–7.
2. Bill Hybels, *Christians in a Sex-Crazed Culture* (Wheaton, IL: Victor Books, 1989), 62.
3. David Mace, *Whom God Has Joined* (Rev. Ed.), (Philadelphia: The Westminster Press, 1973), 41, 44.

CHAPTER SIXTEEN

1. Patty Roberts, *Ashes to Gold* (Waco, TX: Word Books, 1983), 70–71.
2. Bill and Pam Farrel, Jim and Sally Conway, *Pure Pleasure* (Downer's Grove, IL: Inter-Varsity Press, 1994), 117–18.
3. Stephen Arterburn, *When Sex Becomes an Addiction* (Pomona, CA: Focus on the Family, 1991), 17.
4. Cliff and Joyce Penner, *Counseling for Sexual Disorders* (Dallas: Word, 1994), 38–39.

CHAPTER SEVENTEEN

1. Sheldon Vanauken, *A Severe Mercy* (San Francisco: Harper and Row, 1977), 29.
2. Lewis Smedes, *Sex for Christians* (Grand Rapids, MI: Eerdmans, 1994), 168–69.

Note to the Reader

The publisher invites you to share your response to the message of this book by writing Discovery House Publishers, Box 3566, Grand Rapids, MI 49501, USA. For information about other Discovery House books, music, or videos, contact us at the same address or call 1-800-653-8333. Find us on the Internet at http://www.dhp.org/ or send e-mail to books@dhp.org.